Strong Medicine

-by Bob Michaels

Table of Content

Introduction

This book is devoted to Independent Living (IL). It contains random ideas and lessons I have learned over many years. I will share experiences that made me laugh and ones that made me cry. I will tell you stories that will fill you with pride and anger at the same time.

Here is a little about me. For the last twenty-nine years, I have worked in the field of Independent Living. Before that, I worked for the states of Pennsylvania and Arizona in mental health and developmental disability programs, respectively. In other words, I have always worked in social services, but when I had an opportunity to move from the bureaucracy of government services to the vibrancy of the private, non-profit sector, I jumped at the chance and never looked back.

Independent living (IL) is more than choosing a place to live. It is a philosophy, a movement, a corporate structure, a lifestyle, and a desired outcome. My first step into the IL world was an appointment as executive director of a center for independent living (CIL) called Arizona Bridge to Independent Living, or ABIL. Imagine my surprise when I learned that, by law, the majority of the staff and board of ABIL were people with disabilities. One of my first lessons in IL, I learned this majority representation of people with disabilities is referred to as "consumer control."

It wasn't long before I discovered that this "consumer control" idea also applied to the people our agency served. Individuals set their own goals and decided how long it would take to reach those goals. Family members and professionals assumed support and advisory roles. For me, this was quite a departure from my past social service experience.

As I learned more about IL, an entire philosophy unfolded. The IL philosophy had emerged as an outgrowth of the *IL movement* and evolved as the movement took hold and grew. A fundamental IL principle was that all community activities sponsored or promoted by a CIL would be fully accessible to all people with disabilities. Another was that nobody should be institutionalized because of a disability.

The seventies was a decade of significant activism in the United States, and IL was no exception. IL advocates and people with disabilities in communities across the country demanded the removal of architectural, communication and attitudinal barriers that prevented full participation. They promoted community activities of all types and sizes to educate people and create changes in attitude and to make people with disabilities more visible as equals.

A highlight in my career came in 1991-92. While serving as executive director of the CIL in Philadelphia, I had the good fortune to lead a group of IL advocates who wished to change the law that addresses IL, The Rehabilitation Act of 1973. Our efforts were successful in integrating the principles underlying IL into the Rehabilitation Act and have influenced how other laws dealt with people with disabilities since that time.

Since 1995 I have been working independently from my home, training people who work in this field about our philosophy and the laws that govern IL. I've overseen research, written papers, presented workshops, helped develop innovative service methods, and taught online classes. I mean to use this book to share a portion of what I have learned and experienced over the years so that the IL movement will be even stronger and more vibrant.

About this book

My inspiration for this book is Robert Townsend, who wrote *Up the Organization*. His book is one of only a few that I refer to on a regular basis. Not only is it a great book to read from cover to cover, but you can look up specific topics and read how Townsend, CEO of AVIS at the time, addressed them. His unique perspective and sense of humor made the effort worthwhile for me over the years. Since imitation is the highest form of flattery, I hope I have achieved something similar.

Most of this book is compiled from a blog I have been writing since late 2011, *The Independent Living Ideal*. It is, essentially, reflections on work that I did as director of two centers, as a member of the SILC, and as a trainer and consultant to the independent living community.

I have categorized and alphabetized topics for those of you who wish to use the book as a guide. When the heading is different from the title of the post that I used in the blog, I included both.

Over the course of the past 40 years, I have modified a number of my presentations. I made every effort to identify those professionals I respected enough to use their original material. Please forgive me if I have overlooked something that you contributed. I'm grateful for your understanding.

Don't forget to visit Bob's blog at http://independentlivingideal.blogspot.com/. It includes everything in this book and more—and better yet—it's all free.

Acronyms

AAPD	The American Association of People with Disabilities
AARP	American Association of Retired Persons
ABIL	Arizona Bridge to Independent Living
ADA	Americans with Disabilities Act
ADAPT	American Disabled for Attendant Programs Today
ADRC	Aging and Disability Resource Center
AIDS	Acquired Immunodeficiency Syndrome
APRIL	Association of Programs for Rural Independent Living
CBD	Cannabidiol (a cannabinoid of marijuana)
CBG	Cannabigerol (a cannabinoid of marijuana)
CBN	Cannabinoll ((a cannabinoid of marijuana)
CP	Cerebral Palsy
CIL	Center for Independent Living
CMS	Centers for Medicare and Medicaid Services
CRDP	Convention on the Rights of Persons with Disabilities
CSR	Consumer Service Record
DMV	Department of Motor Vehicles
DEC	Disability Empowerment Center
DME	Durable Medical Equipment
DOE	Department of Education
DPC	Disability Policy Committee (U.S. Senate)
DSU	Designated State Unit
ENIL	European Network on Independent Living
FAQ	Frequently Asked Question
FedEx	Federal Express
IL	Independent Living
ILA	Independent Living Act
IL NET	Independent Living Network
ILP	Independent Living Plan
ILRU	Independent Living Research Utilization
I&R	Information and Referral
LRI	Library Resources, Inc.
IRS	Internal Revenue Service
MCS	Multiple Chemical Sensitivity
MD	Muscular Dystrophy
MDA	Muscular Dystrophy Association

MLK	Martin Luther King
MS	Multiple Sclerosis
NCIL	National Council on Independent Living
NPR	National Public Radio
OMB	Office of Management and Budget
OSERS	Office of Special Education and Rehabilitative Services
P&A	Protection and Advocacy
PTSD	Post Traumatic Stress Disorder
ROI	Return on Investment
RSA	Rehabilitation Services Administration
RTC	Research and Training Center
SAVE	Suicide Awareness Voices of Education
SCA 1	Spinocerebellar ataxia, type 1
SCI	Spinal cord injury
SILC	Statewide Independent Living Council
SO	Special Olympics
SPIL	State Plan for Independent Living
SSRF	Social Security Reimbursement Funds
SpoFit	Sports and Fitness Center (at ABIL)
TACE	Technical Assistance and Continuing Education
TED	Technology, Entertainment, Design
THC	Tetrahydrocannabinol (a cannabinoid of marijuana)
TQM	Total Quality Management
TSA	Transportation Security Administration
UPS	United Parcel Service
UCLA	University of California, Los Angeles
VR	Vocational Rehabilitation

This book provides a perfect roadmap for improving your independent living program. The author helps you thoughtfully consider what you are doing as an independent living professional and what you could do better. His reflections and strategies set forth in this book are based on the ideas and tools he developed over the years as an independent living director, trainer, and advocate for the rights of people with disabilities.

The cover was designed and formatted by Loren Worthington, ABIL.

Actions and words

The things that people say

Many years ago, prior to the onset of my disability, I was with a friend of mine and she shared a small, insignificant, and harmless incident that happened to her. I still think about it today.

I got on an elevator with my friend, who happened to be in a wheelchair. There was a man on the elevator that we did not know who got off shortly before us.

After he left the elevator, my friend asked me if I had noticed the man's reaction to her. I told her no, I hadn't noticed anything. She proceeded to tell me about something that happened to her all the time.

She said that when she found herself alone with a male stranger (like the guy who had just exited), they would frequently look at her, bite their lower lip or shake their heads a little, and then give her the "Oh, you're a trooper" look.

Since becoming disabled myself, I have gotten used to similar comments made to me by well-meaning people that remind me of that day in the elevator. In most cases, they are innocent attempts at empathy and I simply blow them off. Certain things, however, do get under my skin.

Sometimes I use a walker—one of those with brakes and a seat. To keep from losing my balance, I often put items on the seat and use the walker to steady myself. I can't count the number of people who say how "lucky" I am. Similarly, when I'm using my scooter, able-bodied people tell me they wish they had to use one.

Sure.

What bothers you?

ADAPT

I used to ask students in my on-line classes at what point they had realized that having a disability was more than just a personal experience. I asked if they knew about the disability movement and that they were part of it. Most often, the students who did know about the disability movement said they learned about it through the NCIL March to Capitol Hill or they had been to an ADAPT rally.

For me, it was ADAPT.

Many years ago, I attended an ADAPT demonstration in San Francisco. (At that time, ADAPT stood for American Disabled for Accessible Public Transportation.) I was one of 500 people demonstrating at a conference being attended by public transportation officials. The crowd was chanting in unison -- calling (literally) for a change in transportation policies. I still can't find words to describe the deep well of emotion I felt that day. I was surrounded by 500 fellow human beings who felt just as strongly as I did, or stronger, about the unfairness of these practices. It was my awakening.

ADAPT (now American Disabled for Attendant Programs Today) has been a leader in the disability movement. ADAPT played a big part in moving the culture and policy approach in the United States away from its bias toward institutional care toward a community-based living model. On any given day, ADAPT members are in the faces of congressmen who will not support changes that would make it possible for people with disabilities to live independently. The next day, those same members might be working hand-in-hand with bureaucrats from the Center for Medicare and Medicaid Services (CMS). Part of what makes ADAPT effective is that nobody wants ADAPT members in their face.

ADAPT supports using civil disobedience, meaning that ADAPT members will risk getting arrested to achieve their goals. While this is not a requirement of membership, I can tell you personally that it is good for the soul.

One time I tried to talk the leader of ADAPT, Wade Blank, into coming down to Phoenix for a day. We were going to hold an event at Greyhound, which was headquartered in our city.

Wade turned me down. This is how he explained it.

ADAPT events are always at least four days. On the first evening, ADAPT pickets the target group and several ADAPT members are usually arrested. The following day's news headlines typically describe the "outside agitators" who were arrested.

ADAPT continues its demonstration the next day with several more arrests. Talk radio and other media have a field day, stoking the anger in the community.

On the third day, the media starts talking with its own community members who are people with disabilities and hearing how these issues impact their lives every day.

On the fourth day, ADAPT leaves town and the issue is on the table, and local people have politicians and the media on their side.

An important word of warning: Don't allow yourself to become a media pawn. Almost surely, someone from the media will call the CIL or SILC to comment on the event. If you criticize ADAPT, you will turn attention away from the issue and lose media and public interest. Do not take a position regarding ADAPT – even if you dislike their tactics.

Instead, if you are contacted, be ready to point out how many people are on the waiting list, or where the state is wasting money, or what it is like to be institutionalized. Better yet, have a list of statistics next to the phone that tell the story you want the community to hear.

Advisory committees

Advise this

I discourage people with disabilities from serving on agency committees that are "advisory."

Your time is valuable and joining these Committees is a waste. Agencies and communities often create meaningless advisory committees to ward off complaints when nothing has changed.

The next time you or one of your staff has an opportunity to serve on a committee, find out if the committee has any real decision-making authority or a track record of results. In spite of how the agency responds, it probably does not. Sometimes, you can read minutes from past Committee meetings or talk to current or previous members to learn more about their work.

A good example is a Committee that used to be called the Mayor's Committee for the Employment of People with Disabilities (formerly, the Handicapped). If its last real accomplishment was raising the "handicap" parking signs from 36 to 48 inches, look out.

Advocacy

CILs and SILCs are among only a few entities that are allowed by law to engage in advocacy. As a result of this advocacy role, other agencies are threatened by CILs and SILCs because they point out an organization's mistakes and weaknesses and ask for change. A good advocate is not always welcome, wanted, or liked.

Advocacy, advocacy, and advocacy

About 25 years ago, Ed Roberts was asked what he believed were the most important services that centers offered. "Advocacy, advocacy, and advocacy," he replied, "but not necessarily in that order."

Ed was pointing out that CILs had lost sight of their primary mission and were more concerned about being good service providers than good advocates. His call for change was echoed by advocates across the country who agreed it was time to get IL back on track. Many organizations providing leadership in IL at that time, including NCIL and APRIL, answered Ed's call to action and began making advocacy the centerpiece of their conferences.

This renewed emphasis on advocacy had a huge impact on centers. When center staff were asked about services, it was rare that they didn't immediately say "advocacy." In the 1992 reauthorization of the Rehabilitation Act, advocacy was added to the IL title as a core service. From that point on, it was against the law for a CIL NOT to perform advocacy!

Has your center embraced advocacy?

Earlier this year, I wrote a post called "Injecting advocacy into your CIL." There is always more that you can do.

The power of one

Long before Lucy Gwin's Mouth we had another grassroots magazine called The Disability Rag. The Rag would periodically run a story on an individual who, working alone, made changes in his or her community. Sometimes it was a curb cut, sometimes it was making a meeting accessible.

One person having an impact.

Every time I think about how much impact one person can have, I'm reminded of an incident when I chaired NCIL's Rehab Act committee during its reauthorization in 1992. There was a lot of discussion about using Social Security Reimbursement Funds (SSRF) for Independent Living. During a negotiating session with the US Senate Disability Policy Committee (DPC), it was decided that SSRF funds would only be used to support the VR program, and not IL.

During a de-briefing session with my committee the next day, Jay Johnson, a member of the committee, was upset about this and wanted me to bring the issue up again. I informed him that, according to the protocol of the DPC, all decisions were final.

In a nutshell, Jay called a friend who was a staff member of a senator on the DPC and got IL added to the law. Because of that one call, IL has received literally millions of dollars from states around the country.

One person, one call.

Injecting advocacy into your CIL

Center for independent living (CIL) staff and board members often complain to me that their center has lost sight of its purpose and has become a service provider first and an advocate organization second. I used to say that this is understandable, because CILs get rewarded by the "system" for providing services like good soldiers, but not for engaging in controversial activities that press communities to change.

The following are eight actions you can take to begin turning your center staff into stronger advocates:

- Center materials (brochures, handouts) – Describe the center as a civil rights advocacy organization.
- IL Skills Training – Instead of teaching consumers how to take a bus to the mall, teach them how to write a letter to the editor, travel to the capitol, or share a personal assistant at a rally.
- Peer Counseling - Reward positive behaviors while identifying the negative effects of oppression.
- Information and Referral – Become experts in laws and the legislative processes that affect housing, health care, transportation, schools, VR, etc.
- Individual Advocacy – First assist each consumer to act on their own behalf *and then* work with the consumer to raise the issue to decision-makers.
- Systems Advocacy - Require every employee to be a systems advocate.
- Board Membership – Seek members with a broad range of skills and abilities and who have a track record of commitment to advocacy.
- Collaboration – Strengthen and maintain relationships with civil rights agencies, public interest law firms, and P&A.

Assisted living

If it looks like a pig

The latest trend in congregate living is called "Assisted Living." It would seem that Assisted Living is the perfect alternative for the elderly person who is able to live independently now but, because of his or her age, will eventually need more care.

When discussing alternatives to nursing homes, many advocates point out that Assisted Living is a viable option in their home states. This may be true. Let's not forget, however, the lessons we learned with group homes.

Group homes were created in response to abusive treatment of people forced to live in institutions. Started primarily for people with mental health and developmental disabilities, we soon discovered that in many cases, we were just trading one poor quality setting for another.

Yesterday, the Arizona Department of Health Services closed down two Assisted Living homes because of repeated violations. In other states, advocates have only good things to say about Assisted Living. I suspect that, like Arizona, some are good and some are not. The bottom line is that these are still institutions.

Board responsibilities

The following segment addresses the responsibilities of boards of directors.

Too often, the board relies on the executive director (ED) for 100 percent of the center's leadership. Given the day-to-day authority of the ED, this is understandable. However, the bottom line is that the board of directors is ultimately responsible for the CIL.

The following topics are some common areas of concern related to working with a Board of Directors and a variety of ways to address them.

Board priorities

I am just finishing teaching an online board training called *Getting on Board.*

Last year, ILNet asked me to revise this course -- one that I had been teaching for many years. They wanted me to add a segment on oversight of center finances. Working together, we came up with a worthwhile course and this is the second time it has been presented.

I was somewhat concerned because the content is more complex than other courses my students have taken. My concerns, however, were not justified and I was pleasantly surprised by the positive response to this class.

In it, we emphasize the need for the board of directors to understand and oversee center finances. Naturally, not every board member is a financial expert. For those who aren't, we explained the important role that a non-expert can take. We covered steps a board can take to protect itself if there is a financial problem. We also discussed how a board can use a self-evaluation to weed out members who do not take the job seriously and retain members with the knowledge, skill and commitment to get results.

Hopefully, the response of these students is a harbinger of good things to come. If centers are ever going to be taken seriously, the people in charge need the knowledge and skills to do the same.

PR

Another complaint I hear from center staff and board members is that "no one knows who we are."

It seems people believe that anyone who understood what a center does would be inclined to contribute money to support it. Or, they believe that people with disabilities would be more motivated to use the services offered by a center if they knew it existed.

I used to recommend Centers hire a public relations firm. After all, that's what a for-profit organization would do – and it's not really that expensive. I have stopped making this recommendation, however, because it is not really productive.

There can be several problems with using a PR firm, not the least of which is a false sense of accomplishment. The best measure of a Center's visibility is whether the average person in your community recognizes its name and knows what it does, not the number of newspaper articles or radio spots that mention its name.

If those who do recognize your CIL are not inclined to contribute to it, the best remedy is simply doing a better job. If your center wants to increase the number of consumers and contributors, improve the quality of your services. Consumers talk to each other.

If one of your consumers expresses surprise about your existence, perhaps it's because he or she is finally receiving the needed services.

Indirect costs

As an executive director, I often heard that I needed to keep indirect costs below 15 percent. Sometimes, the percentage was 20 and sometimes it was 10, depending on what was included as an indirect cost. For instance, if I included only the salaries and benefits of the administrative staff, indirect costs looked low. If I included all expenses that were not used for direct services to consumers, indirect costs were higher.

Occasionally the news media would report that a nonprofit organization was ripping off consumers. They would base their claims on the fact that a large percentage of donated funds were not going directly to serve consumers.

Recently, I listened to a presentation by Dan Pallotta, director of an organization that serves people with AIDS. Dan pointed out that we need to rethink how non-profits do business.

He noted that Amazon did not make a profit for six years. Instead, they invested in computer software, advertising, staffing, and other resources the company needed to survive and provide excellent service. No one complained. They understood that Amazon was striving for excellence not only in the short term, but well into the future.

Mr. Pallotta asked why non-profits are held to a different standard. We need to get past the belief that people who run non-profit agencies are lousy business people. Imagine what it would be like if centers were allowed to invest their donated funds to hire good IT staff, or purchase computer equipment that dramatically increased an organization's efficiency. Wouldn't it be great if centers could help pay for staff to pursue their educational goals and increase their knowledge and skills?

We need to stop limiting ourselves by thinking within the traditional nonprofit box. Instead of evaluating a center by how much it spends on direct services, let's instead look at how many consumers are more independent as a result of its assistance. You can start this process by watching the following video. If you are a board member, watching this is a must.

http://www.ted.com/talks/dan_pallotta_the_way_we_think_about_charity_is_dead_wrong.html

What would you do?

Sometimes when visiting CILs and SILCs, I would encounter situations that needed to be brought to the attention of the Board of Directors or the community. This was tricky because I wanted to respect confidentiality, remember who had hired me and why. More often than not, I had been hired to address the very issues that were arising.

Let me give you some examples.

I was asked by several executive directors to include a segment about board member responsibilities and common practices in board training sessions. This segment was included to encourage non-productive members to leave the board. That was easy and appropriate.

Other times, a situation demanded attention. For instance, one time I was scheduled to do a board/staff training starting at 9 a.m. I was there by 8:30 and two board members showed up at 8:50. No staff arrived until almost 10:00 and the executive director rolled in without apology at about 10:30.

Another time, I was scheduled to present SILC training and had been held up because the course materials had not been printed. Sometimes this happened because I had strict accessibility requirements, but in this case there was no reason. Someone had dropped the ball. Meanwhile, several board members who had taken time off from work were sitting around with nothing to do.

To make matters worse, the SILC executive director refused to help resolve the situation. She left her assistant and me to get things back on track.

In another case, a center's executive director had been to the center less than 10 times in the past two years. He occasionally attended overnight meetings in another city, so travel and accessibility were not the issue. His board was made up of people who had been members since the day the center had opened and they often missed meetings. Essentially, they didn't care.

I was never asked for recommendations by these boards of directors. I did have a frank discussion with each executive director about the board's obligation to step up. Unfortunately, they did not.

I'm not saying these executive directors should be fired. However, the disability community took steps to prevent SILCs, RSA, and DSU's from intervening in center business in the reauthorization of the Rehab Act. Boards have an obligation to make sure their center or SILC is responsive to the community they serve.

Admonishing Bob

Shortly after starting my job as executive director of the center in Phoenix, I discovered we were paying a comptroller. I thought this was overkill. (A comptroller is a management position responsible for supervising the accounting practices and finances of an organization.) The Center's comptroller was a guy with no staff and a budget slightly over $100,000. His method of bookkeeping was to keep a few receipts in a desk drawer.

After letting him go, I hired a part-time bookkeeper who did his best to reconstruct the center's financial records. At the end of the first year, there still was not enough data to do an audit, but at least we had some good numbers to begin measuring against. At the end of the second year, we got a "qualified" audit of our finances along with a written report.

I cannot tell you how proud I was of that report! The board was proud too, and felt that we were finally over the hump and would survive as an organization. After that, I could concentrate on other matters.

A couple years later, we were scheduled for another audit. I suspected something might be wrong when the bookkeeper called in sick on the first day of the audit. About 10 minutes after the auditor arrived, she appeared in my office and reported that we had failed to pay $19,000 in taxes. About the same time, our bank called to notify me that the IRS had frozen our account. As if things could not be worse, it happened to be pay day.

Apparently, because of cash flow problems, the bookkeeper missed a tax payment. Rather than tell me, he tried to cover it up. Ironically, we had the $19,000 in the bank, plus a line of credit that would have covered it.

I still can't believe this worked, but I called the IRS and convinced them that this would never happen again. I talked them into waiving the penalties and interest, and convinced them to lift the bank freeze on our account, and put it all in writing.

The following Monday, I had a meeting with one of my board members, the Vice President of Dial Corporation. As we were walking back to our cars, I told him about the bookkeeping problem and the steps I had taken to resolve it. He said I had done a good job.

Later that week, we had our monthly board meeting and I took a few minutes to tell the board what had happened. They were patting me on the back and saying how lucky they were to have me as ED when the board member I had informed earlier in the week spoke up.

"I would like to make a motion to admonish Bob for allowing this to happen." Now, you can say admonish all you want, but I heard (and he meant) reprimand. Other board members tried to talk him out of it, but this guy stood his ground.

I was really, really upset.

I couldn't tell this story for 25 years, but now I do. I share it now because this board member was right. It was important for the board of directors to take responsibility for what happened at the Center and to take its job seriously.

Evaluating the executive director

There was a time in the evolution of CILs that the performance of executive directors was rarely evaluated. This, as well as low salaries, contributed to a high turn-over rate. Fortunately, as boards of directors became more sophisticated, the problem with high turn-over began to change.

Still, boards can do a better job evaluating the ED. The complaints I hear are: 1) there is no formal process; 2) no evaluation tool is used; and 3) performance concerns of board members are not shared with the ED until the evaluation.

In 2007, I asked about 10 center EDs whom I admire to send me a copy of their evaluations. I then constructed a document I call the "**Executive Director Planning Tool and Evaluation.**" This document does two things – first, it documents the objectives the ED is expected to achieve AND it is the evaluation form. The board chair and the ED sign off on both the objectives to be met (at the beginning of the evaluation period) and the evaluation of how well they were met (at the end).

This tool was developed to address EDs with a very broad range of responsibilities, so those who use it may wish to remove some of the tasks. The Executive Director Planning Tool and Evaluation can be found in Bob's Tool Box at http://independentlivingideal.blogspot.com/.

Policies

Every center and SILC should have policies that govern how they manage finances and personnel. Several years ago, I gathered examples from around the country and developed generic policies.

I have placed these policies in Bob's Tool Box. Don't just use the "Find and Replace" function of your word processor. Read the policies carefully, being aware that some directives may not apply to your organization. Different states have different rules.

Bob's Tool Box is found at http://independentlivingideal.blogspot.com/

Being community-based

Every CIL director should take a close look at their center and their community once in a while to make sure they mesh. Centers for independent living are intended to be community-based and to address the specific needs of the people with disabilities who live there.

I used to require executive directors to do a community assessment whenever I assisted them in the development of a strategic plan. I felt strongly that the development of a strategic plan was a good time to look at a center from top to bottom, from the vision and mission to the programs, services and outcomes.

So what does this analysis entail?

The center's mission should reflect the community's needs and the center's commitment to meeting them.

Look at demographics of the consumers the Center's serve. How many males and females are served? How are the consumers grouped by age, type of disability, and ethnicity? What services do they use most? How many are employed or go to school? With whom do they live?

Be careful not to draw false conclusions. For instance, the attendant care rules might prevent the center from serving people under 60, making it appear there is a gap in services at first glance, but not when attendant care is considered.

Once you have a good idea who you are serving, research the demographics of the center's target area. The Census Bureau is a good resource, and there are agencies within state government that keep these types of records. In fact, you may find a resource that has already compiled this information county-by-county. Try your Commerce or Labor Department, or your state Division of Vocational Rehabilitation.

Often the county has done research, the Realtors Association, Chamber of Commerce, and others. Researchers are usually eager to share their work because people rarely ask them for it, and it makes their effort worthwhile. If it's a government entity, it's public information and they must share it.

How about the prevalence of certain disabilities in the area? Most organizations that serve different populations will know the percentages off the top of their heads.

Finally, try to identify what services are needed. Check out the center's I&R's first – what are people asking for help with? Seek out other consumer groups in the community (not parent or professional organizations), especially if the groups are underserved by the center. Talk to them and find out what they need.

A word of caution -- if your area is like most, lots of people need housing, and the center's capacity to provide that service is restricted by law. The center may advocate for more housing, may give advice on how housing can be more accessible, may work with people who are living in housing that is too restrictive, and/or may distribute vouchers. The center cannot own or manage housing and still receive Title VII, Part C funds.

Fix yourself

About once a year, a board of directors should complete a self-evaluation. This is a simple process, but requires total commitment from board members. It is best to schedule this activity as a regular entry on the annual board calendar because there is a tendency for boards to let it slide.

Completing a self-evaluation is an opportunity for the board of directors to take a hard look at its performance. Sadly, there are plenty of examples of boards that become lazy or lose interest in the work and continue to operate like that for years. A self-evaluation could help you get over that hump.

What do you look at? Here are some examples of questions you can include on the assessment:

- Do you evaluate the performance of the executive director on a regular basis?
- Have there been times when the board was unable to conduct business due to a
- lack of quorum?
- Do you monitor financial performance and projections on a regular basis?
- Have you adopted an income strategy that ensures adequate resources?
- Have you adopted a conflict of interest policy?
- Do your board members have a broad range of expertise and diversity?
- Do all members understand the mission and purpose of the organization?
- Do members follow through on their commitments?
- Do members understand the respective roles of the board and staff?
- Does the board address problem performance or actions of its members, including excusing members if it is in the best interest of the Board or Center?

These are a few of the areas that can be explored. The Internet, Blue Avocado, and Independent Sector have many more topics that may be pertinent to your organization.

Board structure

There are several aspects of board operation that deserve attention. This segment will be devoted to the makeup of the board, how to recognize problems, and how to address them.

Being on the board of directors of a CIL

Not everyone should serve on the board of directors of a center for independent living (CIL). Sure, there are the obvious reasons -- not enough time, too much work, burn-out, and too many other interests. Those situations can also occur for someone who is serving on a Board. If you are a board member and this rings true for you, I encourage you to resign while your peers still respect you. Better yet, don't join a board without giving serious thought to the commitment it takes and whether the cause is a good fit for you.

This post, however, is not about that.

This post is about serving as a member on a CIL board when you question the board's principles. The board of directors is responsible for assuring that the center is following a mission that is consistent with IL philosophy and principles.

Unlike for-profit businesses that are market-driven, centers are *mission-driven*. If centers were market-driven (like McDonald's), they would cater to consumer demands and promote the activities that are profitable and stop offering ones that aren't.

Good-bye core services.

McDonald's will continue to sell fat-laden, cholesterol-loaded Big Macs as long as customers want them. They do this because they are in the business of making money, not because they think a Big Mac is good for you. In the for-profit world, what a customer wants, a customer gets.

- If you are the parent of a person with a disability and you believe that your child should not try to live independently -- you should not be on the board of a center.

- If your work involves trying to get people admitted to nursing homes, how could you be on the Board of a center?

- If you support a business with a reputation for discriminating against people with disabilities, do you really believe in our issues?

Let me tell you about something that happened at the CIL I ran in Philadelphia.

The board of directors had several members, including officers, who had joined the board around the time I was hired. They weren't totally comfortable with the changes we were making, but seemed to go along.

Not long after I left, the board needed to fill a vacant spot. The existing members made a unilateral decision to nominate a man who was a high-level manager at a local nursing home. This nursing home called itself a "rehab center," but in reality a lot of young people with disabilities were warehoused in the facility.

23

The Center staff and its consumers were flabbergasted. Whether this man was qualified or not -- I don't know. But the action was seen as one more example of how out-of-touch these board members were.

On the night of the board meeting to consider the appointment, a large number of consumers took over the room and stopped the meeting. They demanded the resignations of these board members and, apparently, most of them complied.

To this day, the center continues to be one of the strongest in the country and there is no doubt about who is in charge.

Letting absentee board members go

Sooner or later every board has this problem. One or more of the members misses a number of the meetings. Sometimes it results in a lack of quorum, and other times it just sends a negative message to the rest of the board. Sometimes it does both.

More often than not, the people who do this are just burnt out and feel guilty about not living up to the commitment they made. The simplest way to resolve this is for the President of the board to call the member, acknowledge that he or she is very busy, point out that board meetings are critical to meet the legal obligations of the center, and ask the member to resign. If it is someone you like, invite the member to call you when he or she can resume full participation. Don't worry -- the call is not likely to come.

One of the mistakes organizations make is to allow the chair to excuse people who miss meetings. What is a good excuse? In my experience, just about anything is excused.

Once, when one of my board members missed a meeting because her sister was coming to visit the next week and she needed to clean the house, I knew something had to change. We rewrote our policy so that a board member could miss no more than two meetings per year. (Notice that the word "excused" is not in there.)

If the person missed a third meeting, it was an automatic dismissal from the board. We sent a letter confirming the dismissal. If the person wanted back on the board, he or she sent an email or note to the chair asking to be reinstated. An up or down vote was taken at the beginning of the next board meeting.

We did this at both centers I ran. After the initial house-cleaning, we had no problem with attendance.

Board of directors - term limits

I am amazed by how many CILs do not have term limits for board members. These boards become filled with founding and other long-term members who haven't had an original thought in years. Instead of bringing new life and energy to the group, new members are intimidated by the experience of the old timers and fall into line.

If this continues, the organization becomes stagnant. Instead of new ideas being explored and tested, people feel pressured to maintain the status quo.

Experts in non-profit management universally endorse term limits. They say recruitment is easier if board candidates know their commitment is time limited. By planning for turnover, you create new leaders, have healthier boards, and increase fund raising.

If your board does not have term limits, consider putting them in place. The best approach is to add a provision to your bylaws. Here's an example:

> "Each board member will serve one, three-year term. At the end of the first term, the member may renew his or her membership for one additional three--year term upon approval of the Board."

Most CILs that adopt term limits restrict board member appointments to two, three-year terms. You will also need to decide on a fair way to apply new term limits to current board members.

Should EDs sit on the board?

About 20 years ago there was a trend among executive directors of the larger centers to join the board of directors for their centers. These directors were dealing with their communities differently. They had lines of credit in banks, were large employers, and were expected to mix with the community's movers and shakers. As a board member, I was also able to sign some contracts with the state of Pennsylvania.

In most cases, the executive director's title became Chief Executive Officer (CEO). The ED's level of involvement on the board varied from center to center. Some were officially on the board, but couldn't vote. Others could vote, but could not hold an office.

I was not on the board at my first center in Phoenix, but I was on the board in Philadelphia. There were no restrictions on holding an office, but I never pursued it.

As I look back, I'm not sure making the change was worth it. On the other hand, making the change was pretty painless. I'd be interested to hear what today's EDs think.

Is your board boring?

When I was the director of the Center for Independent Living (CIL) in Philadelphia, I decided to add two consumers to the Board of Directors. I'm not talking about making sure at least 50% of board members are people with disabilities. I'm talking about adding people who actually used the services of our Center.

After talking to staff, I invited a man that CIL staff had helped move into the community after living in a nursing home for 12 years. I also added a woman who had been living in a nursing home for 24 years when we helped her move into the community.

Adding these two members had an immediate impact. First of all, it made board members more conscientious about the language they used to discuss consumers. More important, perhaps, was the impact it had on me. I had chosen consumers who were not shy about speaking up. As a result, I learned that some of the statements I routinely made to the board were incorrect. For instance, I made a statement about the transition process that was true for some consumers, but not at all true for others. These consumers were not shy about telling me and the rest of the board the way it really happened for them.

The woman left the board after a short tenure and is now a member of the staff.

Capital punishment

Capital Punishment and Mental Retardation

Before I go any further, I must disclose that I am against capital punishment. I know that when asked, a majority of Americans say they are in favor of it.

Given that, I want to bring up recent debates about executing people who experience mental retardation. Various states are discussing what constitutes "being mentally retarded." In some states, people say that the standard should be an IQ of 75. People in other states say it should be 70. Still others do not identify a particular IQ, but leave it to a court decision.

IL advocates who are in favor of capital punishment do the disability community a disservice when they ask for special consideration for people who are mentally retarded. People who are mentally retarded know right from wrong.

Choice
Supporting a person's right to make a decision doesn't mean you have an obligation to help the person carry it out.

What would you do?

One of the toughest IL concepts to understand is related to consumer choice. Many advocates believe that once a consumer makes a choice, center staff are required to help the person carry out the decision. Many advocates who work for CILs agree.

I don't.

Just because a consumer makes a decision, it does not mean that we must help him or her carry it out. For some reason, otherwise clear-thinking advocates believe we have to abide by any consumer decision, even if it violates our own philosophy.

There is a difference between respecting someone's right to make a choice and helping that person fulfill it. In my training, I present a scenario in which a consumer chooses to go into a nursing home after considering all the options. The dilemma is whether or not CIL staff should help the consumer. I say, "No!" Centers never support institutionalization. Most people I am training disagree with me and do not see this as a violation of our principles.

Consider this situation.

A pregnant woman goes into Catholic Community Services (CCS) and tells them she wants an abortion.

The CCS staff would talk to her about adoption, in-home supports, foster care, and other options. Despite their attempts to persuade her to have the baby, she still wants an abortion. Are they going to send her to a clinic? Of course not!

Helping someone get an abortion is inconsistent with CCS's philosophy. No one would expect anything less. Yet, here we are saying that a center should institutionalize someone because they request it.

What do you think?

It's my right

I use a scenario in training in which a consumer decides that he wants to go into a nursing home. The issue is whether the IL principle of consumer choice trumps our commitment to community-based services. The dilemma is whether or not CIL staff should assist the consumer.

Being a purist, I say "that's not what we do," and send him on his way. Others say staff should help him pack and drive him to the nursing facility.

I don't think so. Certain principles are the basis of our philosophy. One is not more important than another.

If consumer chooses to do something, it does not mean we must help. We should respect the person's right to make decisions, but decline to be a part of any action that would violate our own principles.

Is there a compromise here? Most students agree that assisting someone to enter a nursing home is wrong, and that passing the responsibility to someone else is acceptable. Instead of helping the consumer, they would refer him or her to an agency that provides this service.

Centers are not obligated to respond to every consumer need.

Commitments

Keeping your commitments

One of the down sides of growing up under the "medical model" is that you don't question that others will make decisions for you. From childhood on, someone else will make decisions about your health care, your education, where you live, etc.

As a result, people with disabilities get whatever is left after everyone else's needs are addressed. The problem is made worse by giving the decision-making responsibility to bureaucrats who have low performance standards for themselves and others.

The medical model taught us to accept these low standards and sub-standard services. Often, people with disabilities lower their own expectations about what they deserve.

To me, this is nothing more than a subtle form of discrimination, and CIL staff contribute to it when performance standards are not high. In particular, following through with commitments is a standard that should be strictly held. In the real world, we would be fired or demoted if we didn't keep our commitments. Yet, I've seen CIL staff who do not take this responsibility seriously.

We cannot expect commitment from others if we do not hold ourselves to the same standard. Supervisors at CILs contribute to the problem when they make excuses for staff who do not keep commitments. SILCs do it when they allow those with primary responsibility for completing objectives to slide.

When employees, contractors or even volunteers, make a commitment that they do not keep, something is wrong. Instead of looking the other way, we have an obligation to consumers to train and coach these workers and to make sure that those assisting consumers are competent.

Community integration

There was a time when CILs participated in activities that were exclusively for people with disabilities or that highlighted disability issues in the community. Today, we realize that by segregating people with disabilities, we perpetuate the idea that they are different and must be treated differently. Still, many centers do it under pressure from their communities.

Sometimes, it's not CILs at all, just well-meaning people and organizations who need to be educated.

Disability awareness day

When I first got involved in the IL Movement, there were two fairly common disability awareness activities conducted by Center staff. Thank God these are now recognized as non-productive, if not harmful to the cause of disability rights.

The first was an event usually held along with the community's Disability Awareness Day. The mayor or a city council member would visit the center and sit in a wheelchair for an hour or two. CILs that were really go-getters might blindfold or put Vaseline on the glasses of the victim.

Before long, center staff started to realize that it did more harm than good when the participants actually thought they understood what it was like to have a disability after spending an hour in a chair.

The second activity was a little more subtle. It occurred when centers would host a competition, such as an art show or 10k, exclusively for people with disabilities. Instead of working to open the competition to people without disabilities or encouraging consumers to enter community events that are for everyone, we assumed that they could not compete in a wide-open contest.

Most centers see this segregation for what it is, but other organizations still do not. This is where CILs need to step in and demand full integration.

Recently, there was a story on the local news about a new baseball field that had been built for children with disabilities. They bragged about the accessible dugouts and flat surfaces (to prevent tripping). Other than that, it looked similar to a dugout any other kid in Little League would use.

That's my point.

Why isn't anyone approaching Little League officials about opening teams to kids with disabilities? What if children with disabilities started like their peers in tee ball? As long as society assumes that people with disabilities can't compete, they can't be proven wrong.

Dancing your rights away

Once, while I was at my physical therapist's office, there was a young patient with cerebral palsy (CP). He was a senior in high school -- the same school my sons had attended. I overheard the young man tell his PTs that he had asked a girl to go to the prom with him and that she had backed out at the last minute.

Two of the PTs immediately responded that they would go with him. He declined their offers, though in my view he would have been the envy of his peers. These two women were every young man's dream.

Instead, he chose to attend with a group of students from Special Ed. The girls who "volunteered" to be their dates deserted them shortly after arriving at the dance. Bad things happen.

I tell this story because of a recent article in the newspaper about a prom in San Diego held exclusively for people with developmental disabilities.

Supporters raved about the event because, they said, the kids were able to attend a dance "just for them." All expenses were covered, including formal wear, flowers, pictures, and limo rides. One attendee said, "It's just like any other high school dance, minus the awkwardness and multiply (sic) the happiness."

As you can imagine, I hate events like this. We continue to stage artificial experiences for people with disabilities. Proms are awkward for lots of kids and not everyone can afford a limo. Plenty of kids don't know how to dance and don't escape the dance floor without making a fool of themselves.

Instead of perpetuating the idea that people with disabilities need to be treated differently, why not integrate them into the events that everyone else attends? Sure, it might be awkward for a while, but not as damaging as continuing to play these bigoted games.

Accessible playgrounds

I once wrote a post concerning a community here in Arizona that was building an accessible ball park for children with disabilities. I was worried that this community was investing taxpayer funds in a segregated facility.

In October, National Public Radio (NPR) devoted some airtime to the development of an accessible playground in Pocatello, Idaho. You can listen to this story at http://www.npr.org/2013/08/27/213827534/for-kids-with-special-needs-more-places-to-play.

This playground was created with private funds, but it didn't need to be. The ADA requires communities that are developing new playgrounds to make them accessible.

NPR has put together a website listing accessible playgrounds. If you know of any that are not on the list already, I encourage you to submit the playground name and location to be added.

This listing may be found at http://apps.npr.org/playgrounds/ .

Consumer satisfaction

Executive directors of centers for independent living (CILs) have an obligation to assess consumer satisfaction with the services they receive. The results must be submitted to the SILC and the Center's board of directors.

The following posts include lessons I have learned over the years about consumer satisfaction.

Going viral

A training that Centers requested fairly often is on Standards and Indicators. After I covered several standards related to Independent Living goals, I would spend about an hour and a half on the topic of consumer satisfaction.

I would present what we have learned about *Consumer Satisfaction,* how expectations are set, how to respond to customer needs, and how to resolve complaints. At the end of this segment, I would share data from Greg Newton, who teaches Total Quality Management (TQM).

Here are Newton's results:

Satisfied versus dissatisfied consumers:
- Every satisfied customer tells 3 people.
- Every dissatisfied customer tells 12-15 people.
- Only one of every 26 dissatisfied customers will complain to you. (However, they will tell others.)

This means:
- Every one complaint to you represents 25 complaints to others, multiplied by 12 negative words-of-mouth, for a total of 300 negative words-of-mouth!
- If you resolve a customer's complaint, the newly satisfied customer tells 12-15 persons of his or her satisfaction.
- If someone complains to you and you do nothing to resolve the complaint, the consumer will tell 135 people.

I was always amazed that consumers would tell 135 people about their dissatisfaction. Then I came upon a piece about a guy who complained about a broken guitar to United Airlines. The story went like this.

A musician by the name of Dave Carroll had taken a trip and flown with United Airlines. United had damaged his treasured Taylor guitar (worth $3,500) during the flight. Carroll spent nine months trying to get United to pay the damages caused by baggage handlers. During his final exchange with United's Customer Relations Manager, Carroll stated that he was left with no choice but to create a music video for YouTube exposing their lack of cooperation. The Manager said to Carroll, "Good luck with that one, pal."

So Dave Carroll posted a retaliatory video on YouTube. The video has since received over 14 million hits. United Airlines contacted the musician and attempted settlement in exchange for pulling the video. Naturally, Carroll's response was "Good luck with that one, pal."

Taylor Guitars sent the musician two new custom guitars in appreciation for the free advertising.

Here's the video: United Breaks Guitars

Consumer satisfaction

I think most directors would agree that measuring consumer satisfaction is important whether or not it is required by law.

Many centers send out a survey once a year. Others poll every consumer leaving the center after getting services. Still others send out service-specific surveys to consumers periodically. Some use Center staff to conduct the surveys. Some use volunteers.

To say these methods get mixed results is charitable. It is not unusual to get a 10-12 percent return rate on surveys using these methods.

If I were to run a center again, I would approach this task in a whole different way.

First, I would pull together a group of 8-10 consumers who are representative of who the center serves. Pay attention to ensure representatives vary in gender, ethnicity, age, and the types of services people have received. Once you set the criteria for selecting consumers, make the selection as random as possible.

Invite these consumers to a two-hour meeting and offer to pay them for their time or provide lunch. After assuring them about confidentiality and taking time to establish rapport, ask the group about their experiences with the CIL. These inquiries could include, but not be limited to the following types of questions:

1. Did you feel welcome? Describe your first contact with the center.
2. Was the staff member you first met courteous and on time? Describe your first contact with the staff member.
3. If you came into the CIL, what did we do to make you feel comfortable? Was there appropriate seating or room for your chair?
4. Do you feel your needs were understood? What did staff do to make you feel that way?
5. Do you understand what will happen next to address your needs? What did staff do to help you understand?
6. If you had a friend with the same needs, would you refer the friend to us? Why?
7. Are you more independent as a result of having received assistance from the CIL? How?

Again, don't limit yourself to these questions. Go where the discussion leads you and don't let one or two people dominate the meeting.

With feedback to these questions, I would have a good sense of a consumer's experience with the center. These responses would give me information about the effectiveness of CIL staff as well as feedback about specific services.

The satisfaction gap

Customer satisfaction . . . the difference between what a customer expects and what he perceives that he gets.   -- J.D.Power III

I love this definition because it looks at the service provider-customer relationship from a different perspective. What a customer "expects" to get may be very different from what the customer "requests." And what the customer "receives" may not be what *he or she* perceives that he got.

The difference between what one "expects" and what one "perceives that he gets" is called the satisfaction gap, as seen in the diagram below. (The diagram shows a right angle with the word "expects" at the high end of the vertical bar and "perceives that he gets" at the end of the horizontal bar. The 90 degree difference is the satisfaction gap.)

Expects

Satisfaction Gap

Perceives that he gets

A CIL needs to reduce the gap between what a consumer expects and what the consumer perceives that he or she gets. In future posts, I'll share information about how expectations are set and how you can give clear messages about service availability.

What we know about consumer satisfaction

Before I begin addressing how to measure consumer satisfaction, we should understand certain "givens." The following is a short list developed by a company called Tarp and expanded by Greg Newton and me.

Tarp is a customer service research and consulting firm that helps companies maximize customer satisfaction and loyalty. Here's what Tarp tells us about <u>CUSTOMERS</u>.

- Your best customer is your last customer. Because of research, advertising, bookkeeping, and other expenses, it costs 5 times as much to attract new customers than to keep existing customers. How is your consumer turnover?
- Word-of-mouth is the most effective form of advertising. Businesses measure word-of-mouth and use it to predict the relationship between quality and profitability. Non-profits use it to predict the relationship between quality and reputation. (For example, do new consumers say they were referred by friends who had used the services of this CIL?)
- Most customers who have problems don't complain. Studies find that over 50 percent of consumers won't tell you they are unhappy.

Problem rates decrease when complaints are solicited. If you let people know that you care about their opinion of your services, they will be happier and less likely to complain. Hopefully, it's because you promptly address any complaints they have.

Staff training and product improvement have a high return on investment. Studies report that you can increase your profit many times over if you just train your staff well. Happy, well-trained staff who feel valued are more invested in what they have to offer, whether it's a Ford or IL Skills Training.

The vast majority of complaints are made to front line staff. This is referred to as the "tip of the Iceberg" phenomenon because 50 percent of customers say nothing, 45 percent complain to front line staff, and only 1-5 percent tell management. What does this tell you about the need to talk to the center's receptionist to learn about customer satisfaction?

Setting expectations - closing the satisfaction gap

In an earlier post, I shared a quote by J.D. Power III that I like. He said, "Customer satisfaction is the difference between what a customer expects and what he perceives that he gets."

Consumer satisfaction falls when they have unrealistic expectations about what the program can do for them. Sometimes consumers create those expectations themselves, but not usually. This post briefly looks at how consumer expectations are set and what you can do to alleviate confusion.

The most common source of confusion created outside the Center is by an agency making a **referral** to the Center. Sometimes it is an innocent misunderstanding. A friendly agency that is not familiar with Center services misinforms someone about what we do while making a referral.

Other times, it is not an innocent misunderstanding. For example, after determining an applicant ineligible for services, an agency staff person sometimes refers the person to a center for "whatever assistance they need" as a way to ease the guilt about denying services to the individual.

A good practice is to ask each new consumer what agency referred them to the Center, and to keep track of these referral sources. A smart center will visit agencies that make the most referrals and educate its staff about the center's services, eligibility process, and limitations.

Another source of confusion for consumers may be the CIL's **marketing materials**. Read through them carefully. If any of your services are limited, say so. For example, if you have a home modification program, but only for low income consumers, don't make it sound like it's available for all consumers.

Past consumers can set expectations as well. While it is always pleasing to have consumers say nice things about the center, it isn't helpful if they don't understand why they received a certain kind of assistance. Using the home modification example, make sure this consumer understands why he or she qualifies for the service so they don't misdirect an unqualified consumer.

Initial Staff Presentations and **Program Orientations** can also be sources of confusion. Not all centers do an orientation for new consumers, but if you do -- be careful. The tendency is to explain every service. It is better *not* to discuss those services that are not available to everyone in a group setting. Instead, provide a general overview of services available to everyone and have service-specific handouts available to give eligible consumers.

The goal is to make sure service options and limitations are clearly and accurately explained by center staff. Centers should strive to close the gap between a consumer's expectations and what the consumer "perceives that he gets."

Consumer Satisfaction: Expectation = Perception

Consumer satisfaction is when a person's expectation matches what he perceives that he gets. How might this look on our satisfaction gap chart? A single line is created because expectation coincides with perception.

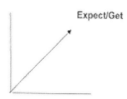

So, how do we know we achieved this perfect match? How about if we communicate with the consumer? (Ask him.) CIL staff must start asking consumers if they are more independent as a result of receiving CIL services.

There are several formal opportunities to do this. Let's assume you have cleaned up your referral and orientation processes and the person knows exactly what service he wants. You need to develop a Consumer Service Record (CSR), perhaps an Independent Living Plan (ILP), and a finalized CSR where you note whether you achieved the goals set. This is when the consumer acknowledges that he has received the agreed-upon service.

Let's say a person calls your Information and Referral (I&R) service. This person probably is not a consumer and, therefore, has no CSR. Yet, it is possible that the person may be called and asked about the assistance she received. One way for the staff member to handle this is to not hang up until the person acknowledges that her question has been answered.

Core services

The Rehabilitation Act of 1973 is the law that governs the provision of IL services. Nothing in the Rehabilitation Act requires core services to be provided in a certain way or over a certain time period. For instance, there is no rule saying that you have to provide IL Skills Training over a 12 month period. Centers can do whatever makes sense for their consumers and can use Part C funds to pay for it.

When I was director of the CIL in Philadelphia we decided to participate in a community-based transition conference in Harrisburg, Pennsylvania. Each center was asked to target consumers who were living in institutions (usually nursing homes) and consumers who had once lived in institutions but were now living in the community. As I recall, we arranged participation for about 12 from each group, plus 10-20 staff.

IL Specialists at the center were required to prepare an Independent Living Plan (ILP) for each consumer who was participating. They were asked to identify goals consumers might address that weekend, such as using public transportation, sharing attendant services, using public lodging, handling money, eating in restaurants, etc.

In addition, the staff members addressed consumer problems, provided counseling, and shared information. The conference agenda was packed with advocacy training and culminated with a march to the capitol building. We asked staff members to track and document all consumer interactions.

The next week we asked staff to complete the ILP for each consumer and discovered that we had provided more units and hours of service in one weekend than we had over the entire previous year.

We continued to provide services to many of those consumers, but the event was a great investment. Sure, it cost a lot from the Part C budget, but it was within our legal authority to spend the funds, our consumers loved it, and boy did they learn a lot!

Think outside the box.

Development director

Hire a Development Director?

Shortly after a new center is started, you quickly learn that you do not have enough revenue to do all the wonderful things your community would like. Soon, the executive director is commiserating with the board, and before long someone will suggest hiring a development director.

Usually someone will suggest that you pay this person based on the money they raise. Maybe it's a percentage or maybe it's a set amount. Either way, look out! Hiring a development director may be the worst step a new center can take.

Not too long ago, accepting a commission was considered unethical. Don't consider hiring a development director unless you have enough money set aside to pay the person's salary.

Before taking this step, however, think it through.

How will a development director fit into the center? A serious fund raiser will need to nurture relationships with corporate big-wigs, meet them for lunch, and attend their events.

The director will most likely be paid more than the other staff, dress better, drive a nicer car, and have an expense account. Don't kid yourself. Other employees will know this and if the director is not getting results, they will resent it.

Nobody is going to be able to raise serious money unless your CIL has a glowing reputation in the community. Your programs need to be seen as top-notch and your volunteers, newsletters and print material must project a positive image of the center.

Before hiring someone who will need to communicate the important work of the center, consider the following:

- What do consumers say when asked about the services they receive from the center -- or do you bother to ask them?

- What do volunteers say about the organization of the center? Can you brag about the number of volunteers at your center? If not, why?

- Does the agency newsletter look like it was run off in someone's garage? For many in the community, this is the face of your CIL. You need to decide who you are trying to influence and the best way to do it.

- What do people hear or see when they first contact the center? Do they feel welcomed? Are calls returned quickly? Are they put in touch with people who can answer their questions?

Before your center hires a development director, make sure the center and staff are ready to deliver on what is being advertised.

You do not want to end up paying a development director to prepare your newsletter and run your volunteer program. Instead of hiring a full-time development director, try contracting with one as a consultant.

Diversity

Again racism raises its ugly head

There are lessons CILs can learn from Ferguson, Missouri.

When a small town in Missouri has a racial blow-up, it's time to look at the root of the problem. About 66 percent of the population of Ferguson is African American. Yet, only three out of 52 policemen (less than 6 percent) are African American. You can't resolve problems if people believe that calling the police will make things worse.

What can centers learn from this situation?

Having people who speak the language, pray to the same God, or even share a culture is not enough. Members of minority populations need to see people from their own minority group when they come in contact with your organization, whether African American, Hispanic, disabled or another group.

If you are serious about diversity, you need to hire members of minority populations who live in your community. No excuses.

Dress codes

Once in a while my staff would ask if we had a dress code. (We didn't.) I used to tell them that they should dress "appropriately." When they asked what "appropriate" was, I told them to use common sense and that I would let them know if there was a problem.

I told them to dress appropriately for their job. Experts claim that people expect those in authority (teachers, trainers, consultants, and professionals) to look...well... authoritative.

I explained it this way based on research I had read: think of a continuum from 1 to 10. A "one" on the continuum is a person who is disheveled and unkempt, and a 10 is a person who is dressed in a tuxedo or evening dress. Consumers want those providing services to them to dress about two steps above them.

So, if consumers dress at about a four, staff should dress at a six. If consumers are at six, the staff members should be at eight. In other words, if a consumer wears jeans and a tee shirt, staff might wear Dockers and a shirt with a collar--not a suit.

Consumers deserve to be treated with the same respect as any other person receiving a service. Do you make an exception for a staff member who is going fishing with a consumer? Of course!

My experience is that people who complain about dressing professionally do so out of self-interest. They say "consumers don't care" to justify their own preference for more "casual" clothing.

Exceptional boards

Board members often recruit friends to serve with them on the board. To protect their friendship, these members can then be hesitant to suggest ideas outside the group's comfort zone or that others might see as outrageous. Consequently, a center can continues to operate below its capacity and ability year after year.

Regardless of how members join the board, they have an obligation to the community to seek out and propose innovative ideas that improve services and outcomes for people with disabilities.

Don't let past successes or failures guide you. Ask why an effort did or didn't work. Propose taking steps to build on programs and make them more successful.

Membership programs: do they work?

Some Centers for Independent Living offer memberships to community business leaders, organizations and/or IL consumers. The purpose of a membership program is to raise funds for the Center and/or to increase visibility. Memberships are usually offered on a sliding scale depending on the type of membership. A consumer membership would be a nominal fee and a corporate membership would be more significant.

The first decision you need to make in implementing a membership program is whether or not you want it to be a money-maker. If you do, then you need to present it differently to your consumers and the community than you would if you just want people to join your organization.

For instance, if you do not intend to use memberships to raise funds, make sure that potential members know that they will be invited to member-only events, will be eligible for recognition, or will have first choice in how to participate in high-visibility agency projects. Maybe it's something else altogether--an award ceremony or access to a speaker or presenter at an event.

In most cases, memberships are not money-makers. They are merely ways for the community to show its support of your programs. That's okay. You just need to keep your goals in perspective.

Must be lucky

A state asks a center director to expand the center's Transitioning program, resulting in a $3 million increase.

A for-profit agency asks a CIL to be one of its Personal Assistant Services (PAS) program providers, increasing the center's budget by $4 million.

A university invites a center to join in a $750,000 research project.

A federal department offers a center $500,000 to participate in a pilot program to inform consumers about a new federal program.

The Wounded Warrior Project gives a $200,000 grant (one of only seven) to a center because of its service to vets.

There is a tendency to look at the success of these centers as a lucky break. That is not so. Each of these centers established themselves as an authority in a specific area. When it came time to increase opportunities, these centers were the logical choices for expansion.

Luck is where preparation meets opportunity.

If your center is interested in becoming an expert, it's up to you. If you establish yourself as an expert, good things will follow.

Serving those who have served us

For about 10 years, centers have been attempting to expand services to veterans. They have educated themselves about amputation, brain injury, and post-traumatic stress disorder (PTSD). They've become familiar with the medications used to treat these disabilities. They've collaborated with other organizations that serve these vets.

Traditional center services do not work. Most vets who want counseling will look to other vets at vet centers. Same goes for skills training, housing, and education.

Recently, ABIL's Sports and Fitness Center (SpoFit) started a series of programs for veterans and their families. Vets can access all areas of the facility and attend fitness classes, events, and activities. SpoFit also hosts clinics, activities and special events designed for veterans and their families. They have an aggressive scholarship program that provides veterans with disabilities and wounded warriors access to adaptive fitness, recreation and sports programs at little to no cost.

SpoFit currently serves 200 veterans and their family members. In the past year, they served over 100 veterans through community transition programs, and over 450 veterans visited the facility. They provided a variety of skills clinics, including rock wall climbing, SCUBA, triathlon and biathlon training, sit volleyball and swimming.

Recently, SpoFit became one of only seven Program Providers in the country for the Wounded Warrior Project. This program serves a targeted population of veterans specifically for the Wounded Warrior Project. SpoFit's Program provided a family camping experience in Prescott, AZ, for 20 wounded warriors and their family members. There were activities for adults and youth, including horseback riding and rock climbing. One of their recreation therapists attended to facilitate youth-oriented activities for the warriors' younger children.

Sure, not every center has a sports and fitness center, but notice the number of events that included families? Notice how many of the activities were ones that would appeal to young, vibrant men and women?

Imagine what the games will be like when these vets begin to play quad rugby.

Nothing ventured

When I was running the center in Phoenix, I received a flyer in the mail advertising that violinist Itzhak Perlman would be playing with the Phoenix Symphony. Perlman is regarded as one of the preeminent violinists of the 20th and early 21st century. Perlman also contracted polio when he was four years old.

I wrote him a nice letter, telling him about the center and inviting him to visit. You can imagine my surprise when I received a call from his assistant saying he would love to join us.

Someday I will tell you about the event itself, which was frightening at first. It ended up being tasteful and a real feather in the disability community's cap. I also received a nasty call from the executive director of the Symphony who thought I had invaded his territory. Tsk-tsk.

One of the lessons I learned from this experience is that we should never assume that IL has nothing to offer. We do. Until we start believing that we deserve praise for the work we do, and the impact we make on peoples' lives, IL will always be on the outside looking in.

Take a chance. Nothing ventured, nothing gained.

Emergency Preparedness

Tony DiRienzi was the executive director of the Arizona SILC for many years. One of the most significant eye openers for Tony was his participation in a practice emergency preparedness exercise.

Tony, who was in a motorized wheelchair, was left out in the middle of the desert while firemen made sure that horses were hauled away to safety.

This single event turned Tony into an advocate, and eventually an expert in this field.

Seven things

Rather than wait until disaster strikes, here are seven steps you can take to impact your community's emergency preparedness.

1. Involve your CIL in the process. Find out who is in charge of emergency preparedness in the community and ask to be part of the team. (Demand, if necessary.)

2. Make sure shelters are accessible. Find out where the current shelters are and find out if they are ADA compliant. Maybe it's time to move to the new high school.

3. Become the community's source of information about functional needs. What happens when you separate a person from his wheelchair? Or when you remove a person from her home, but leave her medicine behind? Or bring a person in a wheelchair to a shelter that does not have accessible bathrooms?

4. Equip each shelter with disaster kits. Supplies might include extension cords, portable ramps, signage, and more.

5. Participate in practice drills. Have people with a variety of disabilities take part and give feedback to planners.

6. Develop individualized lists. Work with each consumer to prepare a list of items to take along if evacuated. Encourage consumers to put together an emergency kit of supplies they will need if away from home, such as medicine, catheters, batteries, battery chargers, etc.

7. Develop an attitude. Do not allow people with disabilities to be overlooked.

Emergency preparedness

As we have seen in recent years, all states are vulnerable to natural or man-made disasters. In Arizona, we may not have tornadoes, hurricanes, or floods, but we do have forest fires. We also have a nuclear power plant and several dams that produce electricity and reduce the effects of drought. Arizona, like any other state, is a disaster waiting to happen.

The Arizona SILC, under the direction of Executive Director Tony DiRienzi, has taken the lead in addressing Emergency Preparedness in this state. We do this not as an objective in our SPIL, but as a project of our non-profit entity. Last year, Tony gave 59 presentations statewide, many through a contract the SILC has with the Arizona Department of Health Services.

The purpose of these trainings is to improve the understanding of functional needs and how they impact disaster response, and to support the integration of necessary equipment and tools in disaster planning.

So, how did we do with the Yarnell Hill Fire? (Readers may remember that this is the tragic fire in which 19 of our brave firefighters lost their lives.) Reports at this stage are still sketchy, but here is what we know so far:

- Two shelters were opened by Red Cross – one at Yavapai Community College and one at Wickenburg High School. Both are ADA compliant and accessible, and each has services to house and care for household pets and service animals.
- Two shelter-support 'quick go-kits' were sent to each shelter. They contain some durable support equipment, portable ramps, extra electrical cords with multi-plugs, a large electronic sign board, etc.
- State Health did their first deployment of reclining chair/beds and some toilet seat risers.
- At its peak, there were 41 evacuees overnight at Yavapai College and 7 overnight at Wickenburg High School. Red Cross reports they had a few evacuees at each shelter with minor access issues that were mostly weight related (which initiated the request for more robust/accessible cots). They had a couple evacuees with cognitive issues and the Red Cross shelter nurses were able to help them with their medications.

We're not perfect, but we're getting there.

Exit interviews

If I ran an organization again, I would conduct an exit interview anytime an employee left the agency. This is a great opportunity to get an honest picture of your agency from someone who has nothing to lose. It's a chance to find out what you do well and what you need to improve.

Ask why the employee is leaving and whether he or she raised concerns before deciding to leave. If so, ask whether the employee received a response.

Ask what they valued and what they disliked about the job or agency, if the expectations of their job were clear and reasonable, and how the employee felt the agency treated its consumers.

And don't forget about liability. Check to make sure any job injuries were dealt with appropriately and that he/she has received all compensation due.

Ask if the agency provided accommodations needed? Some organizations actually have employees sign a form before they leave.

The list of questions can go on and on. Here is a link to an article that will give you more information and ideas:

http://humanresources.about.com/od/whenemploymentends/a/exit_interview.htm

Free will

Doing What Comes Naturally

I do not believe in free will. This, of course, flies in the face of most organized religions and people's personal beliefs. After all, how can you criticize someone's behavior if they have no choice?

My feeling is that a person's action is the result of a series of experiences and that those experiences, when added together, force a logical, inevitable outcome.

Take the example of a guy who chooses to remain in a nursing home rather than move into the community. By the time he makes his decision, this man has been influenced by those around him and has had a myriad of experiences. He will make his decision based upon these influences.

My rejection of free will goes further. I believe that a person who murders someone does so because he or she has no choice. The decision to take someone's life is logical to that person based on their past experiences. I'm not saying that murderers should not be locked away, just that we take these influences into consideration during sentencing.

The same may be said for the woman who gets an abortion or the teenager who bullies someone or a stockbroker who cheats his or her clients. We may not agree with their choices, but we need to try to understand what influenced their actions.

Good Intentions

This section is devoted to those people who mean well, but because of some past
influence continue to do things that keep people with disabilities down.

Athlete robs homeless man's future

This morning the radio played a story about politicians who were taking a class to learn how to talk to women. My first thought was that if you need to take a class, it's probably too late.

About the same time, I was reading the newspaper and there was an article about a group home being built to house 24 individuals with developmental disabilities. Where I come from, we call this an institution. The problem with this particular institution is that it's being partially funded by Kurt Warner, the quarterback who led Arizona to the Super Bowl. Is it too late for him, too?

It's not like Warner doesn't know better. He acknowledges that advocates are likely to have a problem with such a large number of residents. He's not worried, however, because he is not using government money. That way, he can avoid government regulations that would limit the number of residents.

Warner is modeling the facility after an institution in Missouri that houses his adult stepson. He says he likes this setup because, "I wanted to kind of control it."

Indeed. And therein lies the problem.

Growing up

An issue I often address in this blog is our tendency to treat people with disabilities like children -- especially people with developmental disabilities. I suppose this has something to do with the culture in which we were raised.. You remember what people used to say, right? "He has the mind of a three-year-old."

Now we know that this is a bunch of garbage. If you treat and talk to someone like a three-year-old, he or she is going to act and sound like a three-year-old. We are doing these consumers a disservice when we allow ourselves to slip into this behavior.

The soft bigotry of low expectations

I have a dilemma. I believe that affirmative action is a good practice because it allows people who are qualified, but might otherwise be excluded, to participate. On the other hand, it feeds bigoted ideas about the qualifications of those who benefit from these policies.

My problem, however, is with a third group -- those who believe in affirmative action and who have grown up amid prejudice. I'm referring to people who establish quotas, allow unqualified students to pass to the next grade, and even reward people who are underachieving.

The road to hell is paved with good intentions.

I don't know who first said it, but calling this "the soft bigotry of low expectations" is appropriate. These people mean well and would never accept the notion that they carry the same prejudices of their racist friends.

How does this show up in the disability community – look at graduation requirements or who waiters look to when taking an order. Perhaps more subtle, we also set lower expectations when we make assumptions about people's sexuality, relationships, or ability to plan for the future.

Why do VR counselors discourage people with disabilities from getting advanced degrees? Why do some doctors advise people with disabilities against looking for a job? Why do we assume that couples with significant disabilities shouldn't marry?

Perhaps it's because the people we know and trust hold the same biases as our adversaries.

Segregation

I have addressed segregation many times in my blog. It is one of the primary ways that those in power keep people with disabilities "in their place." Whether it is in the workplace, education, housing or recreation, people with disabilities continue to be separated from their peers. As said in another civil rights movement, "Separate is not equal."

Usually, segregation is just one aspect of a program that is repugnant. Often, you also see paltry wages, burnt-out teachers, over-bearing parents, gimp ghettos, and contrived friendliness.

It is important that we keep segregation at the forefront of our consciousness. We must continually ask ourselves if we are doing anything that promotes this separation. Do you support the creation of disabled-only art shows? What about separate Little Leagues?

It is one thing to attend quad rugby or wheelchair basketball—sports that require unique rules and equipment, but another to sanction sports where the only difference is who gets to play.

Instead of using so much energy copying community activities, why not do whatever is necessary to get people with disabilities to join in?

Treat 'em like adults

Socially acceptable behavior. I've written about this before, but I keep seeing examples of staff reinforcing child-like behavior.

This morning I was working out at ABIL's Sports and Fitness Center (Spofit) and there was a group of about 10 adults with intellectual disabilities who were using several pieces of equipment.

As I was setting up, a man from this group was using a piece of equipment in front of me that required a lot of upper arm strength. A well-meaning staff member with the group approached the man, grabbed his left bicep, said in a childlike voice, "Wow! You sure are getting strong!"

Why is the staff member treating this man like a child? I'm sure the staff member would say that this is what the man understands, and she would be exactly right. As long as we continue to treat our consumers like children, they will act like children.

After the man completed his workout on this machine, he came over to my area and stood uncomfortably close to where I was working out. I motioned for him to move out of my space. When he didn't leave, I said firmly, "Get out of my face." He slowly moved away.

Blaming the victim

One of society's sad ironies is that we continue to produce employees who cannot compete with their peers. This self-fulfilling prophesy is continued when we believe that people with certain disabilities cannot learn. In fact, if trainers knew how to help people learn, we could rid ourselves of sheltered workshops in just a few years.

Socially acceptable behavior

Many years ago, a friend of mine had a severe stroke. He was relearning to speak and would try talking with his visitors. Even after some time, I could only understand about 20 percent of what he said. He appreciated that I was patiently trying and when I accurately repeated a word he said, he would laugh and give me a thumbs-up.

About once a week I run into a group of people with a variety of disabilities who travel together. Among them is a young man, who also laughs and gives the thumbs-up upon encountering another adult. His gesture is different than my friend's though, because there is no bond between him and the people he interacts with and the familiarity is socially inappropriate. Unfortunately, others reinforce this behavior by returning the thumbs-up.

One of the greatest gifts we can give our consumers is to treat them like adults (or age–appropriately, if they're still kids). Too often, people with disabilities (especially developmental disabilities), are reinforced for acting like children..

How did you and I learn right from wrong? When we made too much noise, someone told us in no uncertain terms that we were being offensive (probably one of our parents). Yet, we look the other way when our consumers display deviant behavior in public. What do you do when someone is shouting inappropriately? Or talking to himself or herself? Or not respecting someone's private space?

The least we can do for our consumers is to help them learn socially acceptable behavior. Our society is quick to discount people with deviant behavior and our consumers are already starting with one strike against them.

Greatest fear

Coming out of the closet

When I first started experiencing my disability, I was in my late 40's. As I have said before, this greatly changed my concept of disability.

I often ask myself how different my life would have been if I had started displaying the disability at birth. More than likely, I would have been institutionalized and it would have been assumed that I lacked the intellectual ability to compete academically. Within a few years, I would believe this as well.

But, that's not what happened. My journey from non-disabled to disabled was a larger leap for me than it was for my friends. My greatest fear was that my friends in the movement would think I was making a bigger deal of my disability than it really was.

I had reached a point where I became incredibly tired when I spent long hours on my feet, and I was trying to identify actions I could take to put in a more productive day.

Around the time I learned the nature of my disability, I was co-training a workshop on team-building in New Orleans. By this point, I had discovered that my energy dissipated based on how strenuous my work week was. It was Tuesday morning, the second day of the training, and I was beginning to feel the wear and tear of the workshop. I had flown across country on Sunday and began the training first thing Monday morning. The training was scheduled to continue until Wednesday afternoon and I was already staggering around in front of about 80 participants. I decided that over lunch I would go to my room and, for the first time in front of people I knew, return using my cane. I had purchased a collapsible cane for travel in airports, but had barely used it and never in front of anybody who knew me.

At lunch time, I went to my room as I often do to gather my thoughts and freshen up a bit. I pulled out the cane, sat on the side of the bed and stared at it. As I contemplated taking it with me, I found myself first setting it aside, then picking it up again—talking myself into, then out of taking it with me. I had this irrational rush of thoughts running through my head. What if people think I'm trying to pass for someone with a disability-- that I'm faking it so I will be more accepted by the disability community? Will people wonder why I didn't use it in the morning? Will people laugh? Or be disgusted? What if someone challenges me because I'm using it?

Finally, after setting the cane aside several times, I picked it up and went out the door. As I passed through the lobby, several of my friends had congregated to grab a cigarette before the workshop reconvened. They smiled as if nothing was different (of course) and I proceeded past them to the training room to make sure everything was ready.

When I entered the room, there were only a few participants already there, sitting at a table close to the door. There was one other woman sitting alone at the far end of the large meeting room. I went over to the refreshment table to get myself a cup of coffee, when out of the blue the woman on the far side of the room stood up and confronted me. "Oh Bob, no!" she called from across the room. "Don't do that!" And then she actually said, "You don't need to use that cane."

Now as I look back on this experience, it was really funny. Think of it--my worst fear has just come true. To make matters worse, I started apologizing for using the cane. "I need to use it," I explained, "I have this disability called spinocerebellar ataxia and I lose my balance when I get tired."

All the while, I'm asking myself who the hell this is and becoming progressively angrier for getting into this situation. Finally, as I pulled myself away from the discussion, I realized that this was the woman who was doing the real-time captioning for our deaf students. She had considerable experience as a court recorder, but obviously little in the disability world. I'm confident that this would never happen again without me giving her a two word response that would have abruptly stopped the discussion.

Hiring staff

In spite of all the warnings to the contrary, CIL managers continue to use inappropriate hiring methods when carrying out this most basic function of their job. Whether failing to check job references, hiring friends, or ineffective outreach, there seems to be no limit to the number of ways managers can hurt themselves.

Job interviews

About a year ago, I was asked by our Vocational Rehabilitation (VR) agency to participate in interviews for a job opening they were trying to fill. I imagine I was asked because I am chair of the SILC.

On the day of the interviews, each of the three interviewers was given a set of pre-approved questions with strict instructions not to deviate from them. We were asked to score each response and then total the scores to determine the best candidates.

I understand why this method was used. It reduces opportunities for favoritism, nepotism, etc., and keeps the process above reproach. It also, however, prevents evaluating candidates based on *potential* rather than experience.

Of the seven or eight applicants for the job, two rose to the top. One had much more experience working in the disability community, so he was chosen.

There was, however, a third candidate who all of us felt should have been in the final three, if not at the top. The man, probably in his late fifties, was incredibly nervous. He had been laid off during the recession and had been unemployed for several years. He was a guy who had submitted hundreds of applications and only gotten one or two interviews--and he was blowing it.

In any other situation, I would have looked more closely at this man, taking time to establish rapport and make him comfortable. I would have asked more questions and given him a chance to expand his responses. I would have given him opportunities to creatively build on his ideas.

Think of the implications for people with disabilities. What is the likelihood that our consumers will even get an interview? What are the chances that they will be nervous if they do get one? We need a system where we can bypass these rigid hiring systems. We could call it "affirmative action."

Job descriptions

Over the years I have asked centers to send me copies of those job descriptions of which they were particularly proud. I put six of these in Bob's Tool Box in a folder called Job Descriptions.

I will add others as I come across them. If you have one that you would like included, please drop me a note.

Bob's Tool Box is at http://independentlivingideal.blogspot.com/.

Promoting from within

I've always been a proponent of promoting your own staff when there is an opening. You don't have to orient them to the center or SILC, you can evaluate their skills before you make a hiring decision, and you demonstrate to staff that the organization rewards loyalty.

Of course there are times when you don't want to hire from within the organization. You will want to recruit from outside the center if no one meets the minimum qualifications, or if you decide you need to bring in someone with a new perspective.

Here are some tips when hiring staff:

- Communicate. When a job opens up, administrators and supervisors need to address it openly. It is one thing to post the opening on the bulletin board, but much wiser to bring it up in a staff meeting. Is current staff encouraged to apply? If not, why not? If the job was filled before, how is it changing and why?

  If you do not want someone to apply, privately explain why and what they can do to compete in the future. Don't expect him or her to agree with you, but at least you've been up front about where you stand.

  The inability to give bad news is a huge problem everywhere. If a supervisor can't do it, he or she is in the wrong job.

- Set qualifications. Make sure the qualifications for the position are relevant and clear. Does that supervisor really need a Master's Degree? Does experience substitute for education? Be prepared to defend your decision if staff members feel they have been discriminated against.

  On the other hand, a casual interest in one or more job requirements does not qualify someone to fill a position. A good example is when an organization hires someone to "handle the computers" because the individual knows more than anyone else on the staff or board. Many centers have found themselves in trouble with the IRS and/or RSA because their information systems and technology were put in the wrong hands.

- Set fair wages. Staff members need to know that hard work is compensated fairly. If your center has high turnover and staff does not apply for internal openings, it may be that your salaries are set too low. If CILs and SILCs underpay their staff, how can we criticize other employers for low wages? If you feel that your staff are over-paid, you need to look at the quality of your services.

Disabled v. non-disabled

One of the principles of Independent Living (IL) is consumer control. IL advocates successfully got a requirement added to the law that requires the majority of CIL board members and staff to be people with disabilities. However, the law does not say that the executive director must have a disability. Instead, it requires that a majority of the decision-makers on the CIL staff have a disability.

Who decides which staff are decision-makers? The center itself.

When I first joined IL in 1984, I did not have a disability. What I did have were the skills necessary to rescue a center that was about to go under. I also had a personal philosophy that fit IL like a glove. I found there was a significant role I could play while keeping staff and board members with disabilities in the forefront.

I wish I could say that all directors without disabilities were unassuming, but they weren't. Many saw being the director of a CIL as a small step on their career ladder to success. When they left the CIL to go to an organization counter to IL Philosophy—they were frequently replaced by another non-disabled person.

In 1991, I was asked to apply for the executive director position at the center in Philadelphia. When I asked why they were approaching me, I was told that the center had lost track of its advocacy mission and had developed such a bad reputation in the disability community that staff were quitting in protest.

I had misgivings about taking the job because of my non-disabled status, but they were adamant about the need for change. I finally agreed and told them I would do three things:

1. Create and install an excellent advocacy program.
2. Identify and train a person with a disability to take my place.
3. Leave within four years.

That was 1991.

A lot has changed since then. There are many more people with disabilities in director and assistant director positions and who have served on CIL boards. Offer a decent salary and moving expenses and you'll be surprised.

Today, hiring a non-disabled director should be the last resort.

Independent living principles

Following is a list of Independent Living (IL) principles upon which the Independent Living philosophy is based. I developed this list for use in training workshops with the assistance of the Illinois SILC and the European Network on Independent Living. I imagine that new principles will evolve much as these did.

- Civil Rights – There must be no discrimination on the basis of disability.
- Consumerism - A consumer or customer is the best authority when purchasing a service or product. His or her wishes must be respected.
- Equal access – All community activities must be fully accessible to all people with disabilities.
- Community-based services – All programs and services that are community-based must be physically located in a non-institutional setting in the community and be responsive to the needs identified by people with disabilities in that community.
- De-medicalization - Individuals with disabilities are not always "sick" and may not require help from certified medical professionals for daily living.
- Self-help - People learn and grow from discussing their needs, concerns, and issues with people who have had similar experiences.
- Advocacy - Systemic community-wide change activities are needed to ensure that people with disabilities benefit from all that society has to offer.
- Cross-disability – Programs and services must stress the full equality and participation of all persons with disabilities regardless of type or extent of disability.
- Barrier-removal - Architectural, communication and attitudinal barriers must be removed to ensure that people are able to fully participate in their communities.
- Consumer control - The organizations best suited to support and assist individuals with disabilities are governed, managed, staffed and operated by individuals with disabilities.
- Community-based living - No person should be institutionalized on the basis of a disability.
- Peer support - The individuals best suited to support, assist, and guide people with disabilities are other people with disabilities.
- Confidentiality – All people have a right to receive assistance without sacrificing their privacy.

Information and referral

Rethinking I&R

As chair of the Arizona SILC, I have been working with the local 211 Information and Referral (I&R) program. In the course of our discussions, I discovered that Arizona was the last state to develop a statewide 211 I&R service. In other words, every state now has a 211 service.

In Arizona, our goal is to expand the generic I&R service so that it is more functional for people with disabilities, and we are funding these improvements. For instance, if a person with disabilities needs a heating voucher during the winter, he or she should be able to acquire the same assistance from 211 that is available to everyone else.

Truthfully, our centers have not been providing this information to callers who live in rural parts of the state. So, Arizona will be using Part B dollars to expand this information and develop systems that allow people with disabilities who call 211 to identify themselves.

The centers for independent living will continue providing disability-specific information and to be identified as a resource for 211.

This change raises an issue that needs to be addressed by IL.

On one hand, our goal should always be to have community services accessible to our consumers. Yet there are many centers and states that evaluate I&R by counting the number of calls handled by staff members.

Centers should never be evaluated on the number of people or services provided. There is nothing in the law or regulations that specify what number or percent increase is expected. The law only requires that centers provide this core service. Don't we really want to know how many people who called for I&R received the information they were seeking? This is one of the Outcome Measures that NCIL has been pursuing.

If you would like to view more information about Outcome Measures, look in Bob's Tool Box.

Innovation

About 15 years ago, Independent Living Research Utilization (ILRU) started a competition to identify innovative CILs. They took applications from centers that were addressing an IL problem in a new and different way. I was among a team of reviewers that looked over the applications and picked a handful of centers that stood out.

ILRU then paid someone from the center being featured, or someone else in the field, to write a short monograph about their project. The resulting paper was placed on the ILNET website in its Publications section under Readings for Independent Living. http://www.ilru.org/html/projects/ilnet/ilnet_readings.htm

Hopefully, these papers inspired others to "Think outside the Box."

Three of my favorites were:

1. Resource Center for Independent Living in Utica, NY, sold Interpreter Memberships to businesses to make health care more accessible to people who are deaf.

2. ABIL in Phoenix, AZ, developed a system to recruit and maintain a large volunteer base to support their massive Peer Mentoring Program.

3. Kenai Peninsula CIL on the Kenai Peninsula, AK, leased vans to the local cab company after becoming frustrated with the lack of accessible transportation in the community.

Look over the entire ILNET website. Lots of great stuff.

Thinking outside the box

When the Rehabilitation Act was amended in 1992, NCIL worked to influence the law to assure that CILs had latitude in carrying out their duties, for example:

- We listed, but did not define the core services.
- The law gave the CIL board of directors the freedom to set and change the center's goals and objectives.
- The Standards and Indicators, while instructive, gave centers autonomy in deciding how to apply them.
- We made sure centers could not be financially penalized for hard hitting advocacy.

So when I hear that a center is looking for a canned skills training program for consumers, I want to scream. Shouldn't we reject any attempt to standardize treatment for consumers? Doesn't our belief that each person is unique fly in the face of any effort to categorize and label people?

There's no law that says you must spend 1/12th of your Part C IL funds each month, or that you can't charge for core services, or that you can't pay your staff commissions, or that the rates you charge must be dictated by VR.

Of course there are people who will say you can't do any of this. If they do, ask them to show you where it says this in the Rehab Act. They can't.

When I ran the CILs in Arizona and Pennsylvania, I told the DSU in each state that I was charging $56/hour (our real cost) for core services rather than the $18/hour they had been paying. When they swore they would never buy another hour of service, my response was, "Good, because every time I sell you an hour of service at $18, I have to raise $38."

Think outside the box.

Ask your consumers what they really need. Don't limit them to the list of your current services. Find out what they need and why they can't obtain it. This is a great project for your SILC.

Be creative in addressing consumer needs. Maybe it means putting them on a bus and traveling somewhere. Maybe it means exposing them to a new, exciting experience. There's no rule against spending all of your IL Skills Training money in one weekend. Just make sure it's tied to consumers' IL plans.

Thinking inside the box

About 10 years ago I tried to convince centers that we should expand training to include presenting it remotely through the use of Skype. I approached several directors who I thought would be willing to try something new. I finally settled on a woman who directed a moderately-sized center in the West. We agreed that I would deliver training to the center's board of directors one evening for about two hours, and I agreed to do so at no cost. She never followed through with our plans, so the remote form of training never materialized.

I recently started using Skype for sessions with a doctor in Washington State who is into holistic medicine. It works just fine. In addition, yesterday National Public Radio (NPR) did a story about mental health counseling that is offered nationwide using Skype. Think of the implications.

Skype and similar services are no longer new. I don't understand why CILs aren't using these services more. Certainly, this could reduce travel and be a great accommodation for folks who use interpreters.

Institutions

One of the basic principles of Independent Living is that no one should be institutionalized because of their disability. As a result, much of our effort is expended transitioning people out of institutions and keeping those who are already in the community from going into one.

This principle has been integrated in IL core services and outcome measures, and is the centerpiece of CIL staff training.

The road to Hell...

I came across an article called "The Darker Ages: What's Wrong with Institutions?" by Audrey King, an internationally known speaker and writer who also happens to have polio.

I couldn't help remembering the number of people over the years who have told me that placement in an institution was all right because it was the person's choice. Or perhaps it was a well-meaning person who had moved a parent to a nursing home.

The road to Hell is paved with good intentions.

In her book, Audrey King writes about institutions from her personal experience, having spent two years in one when she was a child. The entire article may be found at http://www.independentliving.org/column/king8_00.html

I recommend that you read it because the article touches on many concerns of the disability community. Although the institution Ms. King writes about was terrible, it is by no means unusual.

As she says in the article, the "intent of institutions is to provide a safe and secure environment for a large number of persons with similar needs in a cost efficient, fiscally responsible manner."

It's the "cost efficient, fiscally responsible" part that always comes back to haunt us. Whether it is low wages paid to staff, substandard food and equipment, inadequate staff coverage, lack of privacy, inconvenient meal schedules, locked doors or whatever -- institutions must answer to their funders. The bottom line is that an institution must compete financially and to do so, corners always have to be cut.

Let's not kid ourselves. Leaving beds empty is never the solution.

Ten complaints about nursing homes

An institution is a society, tradition, or organization that governs the behavior of a set of individuals within a given community. While an institution may have been created for all the right reasons, its nature is such that it will deny personal preferences for the greater good of the institution itself.

Nursing homes are institutions. While I was director of CILs in Phoenix and Philadelphia, we moved hundreds of people out of nursing homes and into the community, often back with their families. Rather than try to outline the deficiencies of nursing homes, let me tell you what we found.

1. Bed sores (pressure sores) - This is damaged skin caused by staying in one position for too long. Usually, this was caused when nursing homes had untrained or insufficient staff, but sometimes because staff were uncaring.

2. Locked wards and outside doors – Our consumers complained that their residential units and often entire homes were locked and they could not freely use the facility or enjoy the outdoors. Staff said this was because some residents tended to walk off and get lost.

3. No cooking – All meal preparation was done centrally. Residents were not even allowed to prepare instant foods, such as coffee or oatmeal in their rooms. Apparently, because most residents did not cook, everyone was forced to use the centralized system. There was a rule against cooking in individual rooms because residents might burn themselves.

4. Set meal times – If breakfast was 7-9, people went without breakfast if they slept until 9:30. Lunch and dinner times were also rigidly set, and staff went home right after meals. Disruptions to the schedule were not welcome or accommodated.

5. Keeping on schedule – Speaking of schedules, forget those bathing, dressing or eating skills if you take too much time.

6. Loss of privacy – I can't tell you the number of complaints I've heard over the years from residents who never dreamed that moving into a nursing home meant such a loss of privacy.

7. Lukewarm baths – Water heaters are controlled centrally and set at lukewarm temperature. The nursing homes can't take a chance that someone might be scalded and sue them.

8. Unreasonable visiting hours – There are set visiting hours that cannot be violated, even if you have family or friends who cannot visit during scheduled hours for some reason.

9. Staff turnover – Residents complain that they never know who will be working with them from day to day. You may have someone you just met helping you into the shower.

10. Theft – Residents believed that they couldn't keep valuables in their rooms because someone would steal them. Nursing home administrators blamed residents when they complained.

Not all nursing homes are bad, but sooner or later they almost always have to make business decisions that erode service quality. Do we add staff to address these scheduling problems? Do we train staff prior to putting them to work? Do we pay more to reduce turnover? What do we need to do to give our residents more flexibility?

If money is not a consideration, these are relatively easy problems to address. Unfortunately, money is always a consideration, so you cut staff, pay them less, and set rules to make their jobs easier at the expense of residents.

Embracing outcome measures

Whether we like it or not, CILs will have to learn to use outcome measures. Centers will no longer be evaluated on the number of people who come through the door or how many hours of service were provided.

Hopefully, the work that the National Council on Independent Living (NCIL) has done to identify outcome measures that reflect the impact of IL services will be used. These measures will evaluate whether consumers are more independent as a result of the CIL services they received.

The 704 Report is supposed to be amended, but it seems this will not be done before the move to the new Independent Living Administration. NCIL will attempt to replace the existing questions on the report with the eight desired outcomes we have proposed. We have come up with 11 indicators to measure what centers feel is important. The group that worked on developing these outcome measures and indicators consulted with the field every step of the way.

Centers need to be ready for consumers to evaluate the IL services they receive. In addition, consumers who have received I&R will be asked whether or not they used the information the center gave them.

CILs will need to identify what steps they have taken to learn the needs of their community, how many people moved from an institution into the community, and how many at-risk people they prevented from going into institutions.

Integration

When I first started working in the independent living field, our center and others typically held events exclusively for people with disabilities. This still goes on today, despite the fact that we have learned that segregated events often do more harm than good.

Continuing this practice reinforces the belief that people with disabilities need to be treated differently.

Hug this

I admit it. I hate Special Olympics.

I suspect that many readers will be offended by this, but I can't help it.

Special Olympics is an artificial environment. Rather than advocating for an adjustment to existing programs, like Little League, supporters create a fake setting where athletes are rewarded for mediocre performance.

I'm sorry--compete like the rest of us. Those that work hardest move on. The rest of us do not.

I also find the reinforcement offensive. Hugs should be spontaneous, not something everyone receives just for finishing. Isn't this another example of "the soft bigotry of low expectations?"

Of course the participants like Special Olympics. I remember reading a quote once that said, "If you are fed garbage your entire life, you begin to develop a taste for it." This is like the woman who smiles when she receives $9.50 for 40 hours of work at a sheltered workshop.

Don't forget that Special Olympics is segregated. Why not create a program for anyone—disabled or nondisabled—who needs a hand to compete?

Why not? It's hard to hold a pity party if everyone's invited.

Intuition

Knowing when to fold 'em

At some point in your life you're likely to need to make a life-altering decision. Maybe you stayed with Mom and Dad too long, took a bad job, or made some other commitment that you don't want to keep. In other words, you find yourself in a situation that isn't right for you.

I took on some work during the recession in 2001 when requests for training were somewhat lean. I should have known right away that this job was not for me. I was hired to help evaluate the disabled student services programs at community colleges in a neighboring state.

One of my first responsibilities was to attend a meeting of disabled student services directors being hosted by my employer. The centerpiece of that evening was a presentation by a director whose program had been reviewed the previous year. She spoke at length about how she buttered-up the review team with treats and gifts before they started the work. This presentation had been set up by my employer, and there was no disagreement from anyone in the room.

As it turned out, this was the first of many disappointments. They backed out of previous commitments and made promises they didn't keep. As unhappy as I was with my quick departure, I was glad to have the experience behind me.

One of the lessons I learned is that I need to trust my intuition. I had a sense from my first contact with this associate that this job was not for me. Another lesson is to make sure there is closure. Don't leave or quit without saying goodbye.

Are you in a situation that isn't this for you? Have circumstances changed? Be honest. Make a change. The people who count will respect you for it.

Karma

When I tell someone about the ups and downs of running a small center, I talk about waking up in the middle of the night twice a month, staring at the ceiling and wondering how I'll make payroll the next day.

Ah, the life of the ED of a small center. No savings in the bank. No line of credit. No slack from creditors.

Shortly after being hired as ED of a center, I hired a woman as a trainer. I met her years earlier when she was a trainer in state government. Since then, she had worked for a religious organization in Kansas for several years and had just returned to Arizona.

One day when I was commiserating with her about our financial problems, she asked me why we were still in business. Obviously, things worked out financially. That was her point. Something always happened to resolve the financial crisis.

Good things happen to good people. I've learned over the years that keeping one's eye on the prize has benefits that extend beyond the individual. If your center is committed to its principles, it will survive.

Know your disability

I just got back from a conference in Las Vegas put on by the National Ataxia Foundation (NAF). I wish I could go to this conference every year, but I don't. I go every two or three years and always leave thinking I should go more often.

There are about 40 types of ataxia. One of the most valuable sessions is called "Birds of a Feather," where attendees get together with others who have the same type of ataxia. I have spinocerebellar ataxia, type I (SCA1). The session is a great way to find out what research is being done and what researchers are learning.

During the general sessions, experts in the field give updates, discuss trends and demonstrate the latest assistive technology. This year, we learned about speech and swallowing strategies, mobility devices, Torso-Weighting, coping effectively with depression, and much more. We also received an update on support from the National Institutes of Health (NIH).

I can't tell you the number of people who ask about my disability. Sometimes these are decision-makers who control NIH funding. Because I attend the NAF conference, I am knowledgeable about research and funding related to my disability.

You should do the same. I have been told by legislators that they are much more invested in working on our behalf when they can attach a real person to the issue. Not everyone can go to conferences, but there's no reason you can't be on top of your own disability.

Language

I used to ask the question "Does language matter?" at the end of Philosophy Training. The responses I got from participants 20 years ago are much different than the ones I have gotten in the last five years.

Earlier advocates thought I was trying to be politically correct and that I was more worried about what people said than what they did. They felt that people should be less concerned about the words people used than the actions they took to keep people with disabilities down.

In the last few years the responses to my inquiry have changed dramatically. No single incident caused the change. Instead, advocates began to realize that prejudice and oppression take many forms and we need to address them at their source.

Kansas University's Research and Training Center on IL recently published its latest edition of *Guidelines: How to Write and Report about People with Disabilities*. Read it and pass it around. http://rtcil.org/guidelines.shtml

Lawsuits

Sound advice

Shortly after I began working at a center, I realized that the agency was probably setting itself up for legal problems. When a consumer was looking for a personal attendant to hire we would send the consumer a list of names. We did not run background checks on the individuals who were on the list.

I called a lawyer at the local P&A organization. After explaining my problem, he confirmed my fears, but he didn't stop there.

As I look back on it, he gave me some of the best advice a new ED could get. He warned me that if I was going to let the fear of a lawsuit get in my way, the center would never do anything innovative. Of course--use common sense--but don't be so cautious that you let irrational fears keep you from doing something original.

Anyone can file a lawsuit.

If you have a groundbreaking idea write it down, take it to your insurance company, and find out what it will cost to cover it. If they won't insure it, maybe it's time to change your insurance carrier. Don't let the tail wag the dog.

Leadership

For a period of about 10 years, I did a lot of leadership training throughout the United States. I initially based it on a training that had been developed by Kouzes and Posner, two researchers with expertise in leadership development. As time went by, I interspersed the training with materials I developed on my own.

I broke the training down into four pieces which I will cover in the following posts.

Grassroots leadership

One of the challenges in training IL advocates about grassroots leadership is that there isn't much research on the subject. There's a lot of information on leadership in general, but most of it is geared to corporate leadership--such as how to move up the ladder in IBM or General Motors. There is very little for street-smart disability advocates, even from other grassroots organizations with similar missions.

An old standby for me is Saul Alinsky, who wrote *Reveille for Radicals*. Alinsky says the only true way to identify community leaders is to have people from within the community identify "native leaders." Native leaders are those people the locals trust, look up to and follow.

Alinsky also said that there is a tendency for organizations to choose people they can relate to and who look like them. That's why advisory groups often look like the person who set the group up-- coat and tie, college education, good job, etc.

John McKnight and John Kretzman, community organization experts, say that not only do the leaders need to come from the community, but they must be willing to invest themselves and their resources in the cause. In other words, you need to develop communities from the bottom up.

McKnight and Kretzman say there is nothing in our experience to suggest that an outsider can effectively organize a community they have not been a part of and do not know.

What does this mean for centers? CILs are community-based and have many experiences in common with their peers in the community. There will be gaps, though, and staff members should never address issues if they have no personal or recent experience (e.g. SSI, SSDI, homelessness). Instead, they need to support the efforts of native leaders. This supportive role is incredibly important.

As Alinsky says, "One of the most important tasks of the organizer, in addition to identifying these natural leaders and working with them, is working for their actual development."

In the next few posts, I will help you identify effective leadership traits and suggest ways to develop them.

Identifying leaders

This post is about how to identify leaders in your community. Later, we'll explore how you can help them build their leadership strengths.

Disability leaders today need to move away from the traditional roles they've assumed in their communities and become facilitators of change. Instead of being the leaders themselves, they need to begin "discovering the leaders among us."

There are dozens of experts who are currently writing about leadership. Most of these are not grassroots-oriented, but what they have to say about the traits and skills of leaders is valuable. I like four of these experts: Warren Bennis, Tom Peters, who wrote *Thriving on Chaos*, and James Kouzes and Barry Posner, who created *the Leadership Practices Inventory*.

When I look at effective grassroots leaders, I see the following traits:

- **Challenges the Status-quo**. If the current process makes no sense, the effective leader has a better idea. I am reminded of the Robert Kennedy quote: "There are those who look at things the way they are, and ask why... I dream of things that never were and ask, "why not?"
- **Inspires others to follow**. Others are so enthusiastic about the leader's vision that they will work to achieve it.
- **Leads by example**. The leader has integrity, is curious, and will take risks.
- **Shares success**. Leaders recognize the contributions of others and see all victories as group accomplishments.

Make sure you identify leaders, not managers. A manager gets things done through planning, budgeting, organizing, staffing, and controlling. A leader gets things done by establishing a vision, then aligning followers to that vision by motivating and inspiring them.

Look at the person's beliefs and core values. A belief is anything you accept as the truth for you. They are those tenets, creeds, or doctrines that you have accepted as real and true for your life.

Leaders turn their beliefs into core values. Values are those beliefs that we hold so strongly that they direct our words and behaviors. We are comfortable telling people around us about these values, and we believe in them so strongly that we would fight for them.

Look around. Look for people with disabilities in your community who have these traits. Maybe they are consumers, maybe board members, or maybe staff. The skills probably aren't fully developed yet, but that's your job.

Challenging the status quo

Challenging the status quo comes naturally to a potential leader. Unfortunately, this type of person is often seen as someone who "rocks the boat," and is never satisfied with the existing state of affairs. Yet, sometimes these people are thoughtful, ground-breaking, and inventive. They love innovation and change.

Critics say these people are never satisfied and that everything is an "issue" for them. In reality, the potential leader is a threat to his or her boss and anyone else who is intimidated by change.

Despite challenges, these people remain loyal to their principles, and their followers remain loyal to them.

So, what can you do?

If you're a supervisor and have a potential leader on your team, encourage the challenge rather than stifle it. Compliment the person for being thoughtful and reward him or her by supporting efforts to innovate. Use your legitimate role as the leader to reinforce leadership in those who show potential.

I cannot tell you the number of people with disabilities I have met over the years who complained that they were shut down when they tried to speak up for themselves. Not long ago, well-meaning parents and professionals regularly discounted the ideas and perspectives of those who went out on a limb and spoke up.

If your potential leader has more potential than actual leadership experience, you need to help him or her recognize these strengths. Start by asking the individual to reflect on a time when he or she was effective leading others. (You may need to help with this.) Point out that we often do something well, but don't take the time to determine what traits, characteristics and skills contributed to its success. As a result, we may not be able to repeat he behaviors next time we are in a similar situation. Make a connection between the individual's insights about his or her strengths and those of other effective leaders.

Our role at centers for independent living (CILs) is to nurture potential leaders by placing them in positions of influence and encouraging them to speak up. Whether successful or not, help them identify what they learned by reviewing what worked and didn't work, and what they could have done differently.

Inspires others to follow

"If you build it, they will come"

Managers direct us, but leaders *inspire* us. What is it that motivates people to follow a leader? Here's what we know:

- Leaders have a vision and are 100% committed to that vision. This vision is an outgrowth of their principles.
- Leaders understand that the vision can only be attained if others have similar values and wishes.
- Leaders encourage teamwork and build trust among the group.
- Leaders give a high priority to communication among the team.
- Leaders trust team members.
- Leaders are confident that the team will perform adequately in their absence.

As Kouzes and Posner confirm, leaders foster collaboration and build spirited teams. They actively involve others. Leaders understand that mutual respect is what sustains extraordinary efforts and they strive to create an atmosphere of trust and human dignity. They strengthen others, making each person feel capable and powerful.

Gallup polled more than 10,000 people and asked followers to describe what leaders contribute to their lives. The following themes emerged:

- Trust (honesty, integrity, and respect)
- Compassion (caring, friendship, happiness, and love)
- Stability (security, strength, support, and peace)
- Hope (direction, faith, and guidance)

Scott Williams, who is the Pastor of a church in Oklahoma City and writes a blog on leadership, cites 10 reasons people will follow a leader anywhere (I've modified them somewhat):

- They have a mind of their own--not a "Yes Man" or "Yes Woman."
- They always maintain a high degree of integrity.
- They don't have temper tantrums or yell, scream, cuss.
- They truly care about their team members personally.
- They are committed to developing and making every team member better. They maximize their gifts, don't micro-manage and free-up their team to soar.
- They always let their team members know where they stand--no surprises.
- They are willing to receive input and feedback from team members.
- They balance confidence and humility.
- They remain appropriately calm under pressure, under fire, under the gun…
- They produce results and success. They're winners!

Are you a community organizer?

In 2008, there were a lot of negative news reports about community organizers. Politicians ridiculed members of this profession as time-wasters with a disregard for jobs that bring wealth and power.

A common definition of community organizing is **reaching out to members of disenfranchised communities, learning about them and their issues, then mobilizing and empowering them to address those issues.**

Not everyone thinks community organizers are useless. In fact, many people hold community organizers in high regard. Many people feel that Jesus Christ was a community organizer, as well as Martin Luther King, Mahatma Gandhi, Susan B. Anthony, and César Chávez.

Those who criticize community organizers are talking about us. This is exactly what we do in independent living. We reach out to disenfranchised people in the disability community, learn about them and their issues, and then help mobilize and empower them to address their own needs.

Do any of you have second-thoughts about the work you do? Of course not! Like you, I'm proud that there are people with disabilities living in our community today who would have been hidden away in the back wards of institutions 20 years ago. And like you, I won't rest until every last one is free.

When I was growing up, the leaders in my church used to praise those who "lived the gospel." They were the folks who cared for those who were sick, found housing for those who were homeless, and fed those who were hungry. I realize now that those teachers had a profound effect on me. I will carry those values to my grave.

Apparently, there are politicians who believe I should be ashamed of my work. Until recently, I wouldn't have believed that there are mayors of large and small cities who don't appreciate the critical role that community organizers play in making their cities more functional.

I used to be frustrated by elected officials who promised their support when campaigning, but had little regard for disenfranchised communities once they were elected. This latest group of politicians doesn't even do that. They ridicule community advocates *to get* elected.

Lobbying

One of the greatest sources of confusion in independent living is whether or not centers for independent living (CILs) are allowed to lobby elected officials. The short answer, of course, is yes.

There are certain do's and don'ts that are pretty obvious. You don't use agency funds to support a specific candidate or party. To me, this is just asking for trouble.

Beyond that, centers have a lot of latitude when it comes to advocating for their issues. A good rule of thumb is that once a bill is enrolled (given a number), you must be very careful to address the issue and not the specific piece of legislation.

Rather than try to give you a complex explanation, let me refer you to two monographs about lobbying.

The first is an article by Jeffrey Berry, a professor in political science at Tufts University, who wrote an article for the Washington Post in 2003. The article is entitled "The law is More Charitable than they Think." Essentially, Berry is saying that nonprofit organizations that do not lobby are depriving their consumers of political advocacy.

The second monograph is one that I wrote in 1998 entitled "Frequently Asked Questions about Lobbying and CILs." I prepared this FAQ because centers were confused about what they were allowed to do.

I remember Ed Roberts warning us, "It's easy to tell if a center's doing strong advocacy. Someone from the state is telling them they're not allowed to lobby."

If you are concerned that your center is doing something illegal, you're probably not. Reading these articles will give you the guidance you need to do this important work.

Media

Since retiring, I've spent a lot more time reading books and watching programs and movies that I never had time for when still working. The following posts are about books and programs I have discovered and how they deal with disability issues.

The self-proclaimed retard

One of the reasons people from the disability community dislike Jerry Lewis is because he made money by portraying and ridiculing people with disabilities. One reviewer wrote that Lewis' character was a "self-proclaimed retard" and Lewis continues to defend that boob to this day.

This brings up a character created by Ricky Gervais called Derek. A TV program also called Derek is at the end of its second and final season on Netflix.

Derek was a character Gervais created as part of his comedy routine. What makes Derek different is that he is intelligent and insightful. While he has several physical mannerisms that distinguish him from the average person, he is constantly coming up with perceptive observations that set "intelligent people" aback.

I'm not sure that this excuses Ricky Gervais, but for some reason I don't find Derek as offensive as the self-proclaimed retard.

Wentworth: Orange is the New Black on steroids

In the late seventies, I was an Arizona state employee and was working to deinstitutionalize people who were developmentally disabled. We started with state-run institutions, then moved to an institution that looked like it was straight out of a Charles Dickens' novel, and then to the state hospital. At the same time, the Department of Corrections (DOC) was claiming that 60 percent of the prison population in the Arizona State Prison had an IQ below 70.

We had no doubt that Arizona State Prison inmates would score low. The problem was that it was impossible to sort out the people who were developmentally disabled from those who were not. The DOC was willing to label anyone developmentally disabled to get additional funding from the legislature.

That brings me to a TV program I have been watching called Wentworth. The story is set in a women's prison, similar to that of Orange is the New Black. Wentworth is made in Australia, uses many of Orange's characters, but is much more brutal.

A point these programs make is that the women are not prepared to reenter society. There are many contributing factors, but housing and employment are two of the major barriers. Our communities do a poor job preparing inmates for their reentry and the recidivism rate is understandably high.

Waiting until these folks are already in the community makes no sense. Prisoners are going home to family problems, mental health issues, and poverty – the same things that landed them in prison in the first place. Right now, our system is designed so that people will fail.

Before release, each person should already have resources in the community to support their transition. Developmental disability or not, if you give someone a real home and steady employment, success is not far off.

Switched at Birth

I can watch streamed TV shows on my computer. I often begin with the pilot and watch the entire series through to the most recent episode. This allows me to catch the Diamondbacks in the evening and watch a series I hear is worthwhile earlier in the day. The most recent one that I've been viewing is called 'Switched at Birth'.

I came upon the show by accident, and have become committed to the evolving story. The show is about two 15-year-old girls who were accidentally switched shortly after their mothers gave birth in the same hospital.

One of the girls was raised by a wealthy family and the other was raised in a single parent home in a poor section of the city. What makes this series unique is that the child in the single-parent home is deaf and attends a school for students who are deaf or hard of hearing. The actors who play the deaf and hard of hearing characters are actually hearing impaired.

I thought at first that this series was going to be another one of those "Gee, I wish I wasn't me" shows where the characters are magically transformed. Instead, the series explores the relationships between people who are and are not hearing impaired. It attacks stereotypes and addresses many of the usual traumas teenagers go through from a deaf perspective. It explores segregated education.

In the second season, the students at the deaf school hold a Gallaudet-like demonstration after the School Board threatens to close the school. I had the good fortune of being active in NCIL during the Gallaudet demonstrations and hearing both the deaf president and president of the student body speak.

In my opinion, the students in the TV program gave up too soon. Marlee Matlin and Katie Leclerc, who play advocates in the deaf school, sold their friends out.

I would be interested in hearing what the deaf community thinks of Switched at Birth and the Gallaudet-like demonstration.

Guilt

I just started reading a book called *The Goldfinch*. It's about a boy from a single parent home whose mother is killed in a terrorist attack. As he tries to adapt, a number of people ask him if he is experiencing guilt because his mother is dead and he's alive.

This reminds me of people who have PTSD. I have heard that many former service people with PTSD blame themselves because their friends were killed and they weren't.

Frankly, I never experienced that. Everyone's experience is different— from the time the traumatic incident occurs, to the symptoms that arise, to the treatments.

Mom

I've been watching a program on Monday evenings called "Mom." It's not great, but I've been watching it because it stars Allison Janney, who was terrific in Juno, The Help, and The West Wing.

Mom is a story about a recovering alcoholic (Anna Faris) who had a child out of wedlock. Her daughter in the series (Sadie Calvano) is now in high school and has recently discovered that she's pregnant.

The central character's mother (Allison Janney) has just moved in with her daughter. Janney is also an alcoholic who, by anyone's standard, was not a good mother. She was in and out of jail, used her child to smuggle drugs, and generally put her own desires before her child's well-being.

What makes this show interesting is the interplay between three dysfunctional generations of mothers.

At first, Janney refuses to admit she was anything but a great parent. In her mind, she did the best she could under the circumstances. (She had been a foster child with no parental guidance.) Although she attempts to clean up her life, she continues to fall victim to sex and drug-related temptations.

Faris is more successful in facing her problems by attending Alcoholics Anonymous (AA) meetings and genuinely trying to be a better parent. Although everyone acknowledges these efforts, she has decades of bad behavior to overcome.

Ironically, Faris' teenage daughter has a more mature outlook on her pregnancy than either her mother or grandmother. At one point, Faris tearfully admits that her daughter will be a better parent than she has been.

The first season of Mom is spent blaming the previous generation's mother for all the family's problems. In more recent episodes, the characters are starting to see that they can't control the past but can try to make the future better.

I relate to this, and I'm sure many of you do too. It's easy to look back at the previous generation in our own families, point fingers, and feel resentful. But there is really nothing to be gained by reliving the past. What we can do instead is create a better future.

We should keep this in mind when serving our consumers. We can help them understand how the past has affected them, but more importantly, what they can do now to make things better.

Bipolar disorder

I have been watching *Homeland*. The lead character is Claire Danes, who you might remember as the star of *My So-Called Life*, which aired briefly in 1994 when she was only 15 years old.

In *Homeland*, Danes plays a CIA operative working to keep America safe from terrorists. An interesting twist to the story is that the character Danes plays, Carrie Mathison, has bipolar disorder. She struggles with her disability because the medication she takes dulls her thinking.

Mathison's way of dealing with bipolar disorder reminds me of a friend of mine who joined me in developing and presenting two trainings several years ago. This friend never mentioned having this disability and I was too dumb to recognize it.

I knew what bipolar disorder was and that people who have it experience episodes of elevated or agitated mood, known as mania, alternating with episodes of depression. When my friend was up, she was great. When she was down, she was terrible.

When my friend dropped off the face of the earth during our preparation, I was fit to be tied. I complained about it to common friends, who reinforced my anger. It wasn't until after she died (from another disability) that I realized what had happened.

I missed my chance to show compassion to my friend and help her through a difficult situation. Don't miss yours.

Ray Donovan: Turning a Problem into an Opportunity

There's an HBO series called *Ray Donovan* about a fixer in the Los Angeles area. He resolves problems for celebrities who find themselves in trouble. Usually, these are the types of problems that would ruin careers and Donovan's methods are often illegal. Because he's very good at what he does and he keeps his mouth shut, he's able to charge a lot of money.

After watching this show for a while, you begin to realize that Ray Donovan is simply a product of his environment. He was an abused, molested child overwhelmed by the suicide of his drug-addicted sister. Despite these traumatic experiences, he's still the most functional member of his family. He does what he does because he knows no other way. He has no free will.

Ray's wife gets mad at him because he is insensitive to those around him. What she doesn't understand is that he has no choice. When faced with a dilemma, Ray will always choose the method that makes the most sense to him. This may seem brutal and insensitive to others, but it is all that he knows.

Behead the dwarf

Last year on *Game of Thrones* one of my favorite characters, Peter Dinklage (aka Tyrion Lannister), was on the wrong side of a competition for his life. At the end of the show, he was sentenced to death. In Game of Thrones, executions are carried out by beheading.

Peter Dinklage is a little person, although on the show his character often refers to himself as a dwarf.

Here's the dilemma. *Game of Thrones* routinely kills off its lead characters, so beheading Tyrion Lannister was not unusual. The only way to let him live would be a complete reversal of every other lead characters' previous fate.

The worst thing that *Game of Thrones* could have done would be to cut Dinklage a break because he's disabled. Dwarfs have a right to be beheaded like everybody else.

Medical marijuana

While attending a disability support group meeting, I learned that some members had been using marijuana to reduce spasms in their legs. I immediately began investigating the use of medical marijuana in Arizona and wrote about it in my blog. Here are some of the posts.

Medical marijuana

In 2010, Arizona citizens passed a referendum allowing the sale of medical marijuana. I have not applied for a card, but I could probably get one because of my disabilities.

I was in a meeting of people with spinocerebellar ataxia (SCA) and we began discussing a problem that many of us have – – spastic or restless legs. We were discussing drugs that we take to address this problem. Mine works at night, but not during the day. For others, none of the drugs work at all.

A woman from Tucson said that her son, who has Fredericks Ataxia, has been smoking medical marijuana and for the first time had been experiencing total relief.

I am inclined to try marijuana. I can't sit still during the day without experiencing restless legs. In addition, pot may help my PTSD. Who would have guessed that my experiences in Vietnam would come back to affect me so many years later?

I'll let you know what happens.

Medical marijuana update

I promised to keep you up to date on my medical marijuana experience. Today I made my first purchases, but I haven't tried them yet.

I decided to try medical marijuana when I was told how much it helped a gentleman who gets severe muscle spasms. Since I do too, I decided to apply for a card and see whether it would help me.

Arizona's process for getting a card requires a physician to verify the disability. The results are reviewed by a second physician and then an application is submitted to our health services department.

Once you get a card, you can go to any dispensary in the state to purchase the product.

When I got to the dispensary, I explained what kind of effect I was seeking. Marijuana typically includes THC, CBC, CBN, and several other "cannabinoids" that impact a user in different ways. I'm not interested in getting high, so I found a product that should provide relief for my restless legs, my PTSD, and some occasional cluster headaches. I purchased some buds to smoke, hard candy to suck on, and cookies to eat.

I will test these out this week and let you know what happens.

The world is going to pot

Before I talk about medical marijuana, I want to give you a little background on my personal experience with marijuana.

I first started smoking marijuana when I was in Vietnam and I continued using it for many years after coming home. For reasons I don't recall, I stopped smoking grass for about 25 years. A little here and there, but essentially I was a non-smoker.

I get severe headaches every couple of years. Once a cycle starts, it can last for two or three months, with a severe headache nearly every day for about an hour. They are called cluster headaches and they make migraines look like a walk in the park. I had a bout of these headaches last summer, so if I'm lucky, I won't see them again for some time.

I get spasms in my legs and I have PTSD. I was told by others who have the same condition that causes leg spasms (SCA), that marijuana greatly reduced their occurrence. Recently, I've also heard veterans say it relieves the effects of PTSD.

In my backyard, we have several aloe vera plants. When someone gets a small burn, we run cold water on it, cut off a piece of aloe and gently rub the gel on the burn. It is amazing how this relieves the pain.

Wouldn't it be nice if I could do the same thing with marijuana-- legally grow one or two plants in the back yard that I could harvest when my symptoms arise.

Later this week I'll tell you about my experience with medical marijuana.

Try it. You'll like it.

If you need to know more about the process that Arizona uses for issuing medical marijuana cards, read my post entitled Medical Marijuana Update.

During my first visit to a medical marijuana dispensary, I picked up 100 mg of lemon drops, a chocolate chip cookie, and 1 g of marijuana called Blackberry. I purchased the three forms of marijuana primarily for restless legs, but I also told the dispensary worker about my cluster headaches and PTSD.

I was advised to eat three of the lemon drops and that I would feel the effect almost immediately. I followed the instructions and didn't experience anything whatsoever. I never tried the lemon drops again.

Next, I tested the chocolate chip cookie. It was a big one— about 6 inches in diameter. I was told to break the cookie into quarters and eat each quarter separately. The worker explained that it would take about an hour for the effects of the cookie to kick in.

After an hour, I was disappointed because I assumed that neither the drops nor the cookie were effective. I was wrong.

The cookie kicked in after two and a half hours. When it did, I was blown away. It was far more effective than I was used to and it took several hours for me to get my act together. I learned two things from this experience--a quarter of the cookie is too much, and it does not provide immediate relief. I still needed something faster acting to address the discomfort in my legs. This brings me to the buds.

When I used to smoke marijuana, I would roll a joint or use a bong. Neither of these makes sense today given the cost and better quality of grass. I decided I would learn how to use a vaporizer (commonly referred to as a 'vape').

I like using the vaporizer because in a few hits I feel immediate relief when I'm experiencing discomfort in my legs. In other words, it works!

I'm still trying to find the correct intensity of the marijuana for the best results. It's an individualized process and one that requires attention by any potential user.

Years ago when I smoked grass, a sophisticated user might have been interested in the level of THC in it. Today, people using medical marijuana should also know about CBD, CBG, and CBN, which are cannabinoids of marijuana that affect different parts of your system. If you are truly interested in the medicinal effects, you will do this research.

As I learn more about CBD, CBG, and CBN I'll let you know what I find.

Mental health

CIL staff needs to remember that the people they serve have probably been subject to many forms of bias and discrimination in their lives. As a result, they have been oppressed and treated as second-class citizens. They may not be in touch with emotions related to these experiences, such as the sources of their anger. They also may not understand why they are unable to accomplish even the smallest task and become easily frustrated.

This is where a good peer counselor is invaluable.

Anger

In one of my online classes, I use a scenario that involves two women who feel they have been mistreated by a van driver and proceed to yell and swear at him. This is a small part of the overall scenario that I added to distract students from the main issue.

Often, several of the students will identify this as a major issue and come down on the two women, suggesting that they should be punished. I caution students that this may be too harsh.

We need to be careful that we don't over-react to any consumer's anger. Many of our consumers have significant psychiatric problems. It is also likely that they have other unresolved issues that trigger angry outbursts. Perhaps the trauma accompanying the onset of their disability or the strain of having lived in an abusive home has left scars that have not been addressed.

We now know that these and other incidents may result in Post Traumatic Stress Disorder (PTSD) that is often untreated. A person with PTSD may be on edge simply because he or she can't get enough sleep. When faced with an incident like the one in the scenario, the reaction seems excessive.

Granted, these consumers need feedback about their behavior, and that can be our role. But we also need to be careful not to treat individuals in a paternal (or maternal) way.

Understanding oppression

How many times have you heard advocates complain that they set up events or rallies to get a message out and no consumers show up? Clearly, there must be something wrong with them.

In a way, there is. Maybe they're oppressed.

People who feel oppressed are less likely to stand up for themselves. The more oppressed you feel, the less resistance it takes to hold you down. The psychological barriers some people face can be just as significant as a stairway without a ramp or a curb without a curb-cut.

All of us have been oppressed. Maybe it was a partner's psychological abuse, a parent who derided your interests, or a minister who made you feel guilty. We carry that oppression with us. Until we recognize and resolve it, encounters or experiences that trigger that feeling cause us to regress.

Imagine what you would feel like if you had been institutionalized--grown up in a setting where men in white coats made all the decisions and people assumed you were stupid because of your disability. Imagine attending schools that you know are substandard and never being able to get a job.

Before some consumers can become strong advocates, they need to get in touch with feelings related to their oppression. The methodology varies from person to person, but if you succeed, they'll get angry. And if they get angry, then you can do some good work.

Is the world less violent?

I was listening to a show called *The Violence Within Us* on the TED Radio Hour. The first three segments addressed why good people do bad things, the mind of a killer, and domestic violence. At the end of these presentations, about 45 minutes into the hour, I was totally convinced that the world had gone to hell.

Then, in the last 15 minutes, they featured a man named Steven Pinker, who made a presentation called *Is the world a less violent place?* Mr. Pinker, a researcher at an Ivy League school, set out to prove that our society continues to get more and more violent.

What he found instead was that society today is less violent than in the past. In spite of the fact that the 20th century included people like Hitler, Pol Pot, and others, fewer people are dying as a result of violence than in previous generations.

Who would have thought?

Where do you draw the line?

More on violence...

Arizona is one of those states where gun advocates always push the rest of us to our limits. It doesn't matter if I'm in favor of gun ownership (which I am). Advocates believe I must also support guns in schools, libraries, and airports.

Last week, a man entered the airport with an AR–15 rifle hanging from his shoulder. He didn't try to pass through security, but did publicly handle his rifle enough to make a woman and her daughter report his behavior to the police.

Where do you draw the line? This man was within his rights to bring a rifle into the airport.

Given the fact that we have experienced massacres in Tucson, Aurora, Sandy Hook, and too many other places to list, shouldn't we be concerned that someone like this might have mental health problems or be intent on mass murder? Should he be subdued?

A man with a concealed gun permit said in a letter to the editor that he probably would have put a bullet between the individual's eyes as soon as the man took the rifle off his shoulder. I'm not in favor of taking anyone's life, but isn't this a call for common sense?

The problem with HR 3717

We're all concerned about gun violence and mental health services. Even Arizona's legislature, which just passed a bill to allow guns in libraries, has given some perfunctory attention to mental health. Along comes Representative Murphy, a Republican from Pennsylvania, who is seeking support for his legislation--the Helping Families in Mental Health Crisis Act, or HR 3717.

Murphy is seeking sponsors for this legislation and Democrats are lining up to sign on. Essentially, the bill expands coverage for mental health problems, including allowing family members and physicians greater control over adults with mental health issues.

The IL perspective is that people with this disability should be included in any decision-making process related to their care or treatment. Of course, we need to recognize that people with significant mental health issues may not always be able to speak on their own behalf.

This problem highlights the need for consumer control of these programs. I don't know about you, but I would like someone who really understands mental health issues to decide how to define "danger to self and others" and not some guy steeped in the medical model. Each state has a Mental Health Planning and Advisory Council. Maybe that's where we should start.

Whether we replace or amend this bill, we need to make sure it doesn't become law in its current form.

Mental health services

When Tucson, Aurora, and Sandy Hook happened, one thing we all agreed on was that we need to improve access to mental health services. We argued about the size of magazines, firearm registration and trigger locks, but no one disputed the need for increased mental health care. Clearly, those behind these horrible massacres were mentally ill.

Yet here we are, years later, facing the same problems. On *60 Minutes* last Sunday, they devoted a story to mental health problems. They focused on an incident that happened in Virginia, but it was clear that the problem is widespread.

Billions of dollars have been cut from mental health in an attempt to reduce our state budgets. No one is saying that we do not need to put our states back on stronger financial footing, but is this where we want to make our reductions? Let's get our priorities straight.

Multiple chemical sensitivity (MCS)

I want to tell you a story about Multiple Chemical Sensitivity (MCS) and Liberty Resources, the CIL in Philadelphia.

When I was director of the center in Philadelphia in the early nineties, it became necessary to double the size of our office. There was space available on the same floor of the building and as part of the agreement, new carpeting was installed and the office was repainted.

I was aware that many of my 50 staff members were likely to be affected by the fumes created by the work. I added provisions to the contract requiring the use of odor-free paint and carpeting that was attached with tape rather than glue.

Although the construction went on for several weeks, I did not have a single staff member leave early or call in sick.

It is not often that one gets an immediate payoff like this. It's not like putting in a ramp or arranging an interpreter, where you see the instant impact of your actions. Taking steps to ensure access that is not directly apparent is less rewarding but equally important.

It is easy to post a sign or put a request in a newsletter not to wear cologne or perfume, but going a step further requires effort and sometimes a financial investment. In 1998, I wrote *Frequently Asked Questions about Multiple Chemical Sensitivity*. The FAQ is posted at http://www.ilru.net/html/publications/readings_in_IL/MCS.html.

There are several actions that a center can take to make the setting accessible for folks with MCS. Some of these are listed in the FAQ. See how many you can implement.

My mentor

August 29th is Justin Dart's birthday. Justin would have been 83.

I consider myself lucky to have been a part of the IL movement when Justin Dart was alive, and even luckier to have spent many hours one-on-one with him. I consider Justin to be the Martin Luther King of the disability rights movement.

Justin would hate to hear me say that. He held MLK in the highest regard and felt that to mention his name in the same breath as MLK's was inappropriate and offensive.

I don't agree.

Not only did Justin oversee the writing of the first document calling for the ADA, he visited every state, rallied grassroots advocates, and met personally with decision-makers. I'll never forget when we took over the Speaker of the House's office at the Capitol. The lead staff member to the Speaker told me that next to the National Rifle Association, the disability community had the most powerful presence on the Hill. Justin deserves the credit for that presence.

My fondest memories of Justin were more personal. He and I found ourselves sitting together on two separate occasions—the first in Washington, D.C., in the late eighties and the second in Harrisburg, Pennsylvania, about 10 years later.

I was in Washington, D.C., trying to sort out my role in IL. Even though I loved the movement, as a non-disabled person I felt that I needed to take a secondary role. Justin said, "No." He was emphatic that I had too much to offer to sit back and deprive the movement of my skills. Justin assured me that as long as I followed the philosophy, we would all benefit. Justin had faith in me when many others (including me) did not.

Justin, Yoshiko and I ran into each other dozens of times over the next decade, but the next time Justin and I met one on one was in Harrisburg.

By the second meeting, our conversation was different. Justin asked my thoughts on the center network in Pennsylvania, how NCIL was doing, CILs' understanding of the need to transition people out of nursing homes, and changes needed in the '92 reauthorization of the Rehab Act. Justin had been fired from his position as RSA Commissioner for demanding many of these changes. Clearly, I had grown professionally and Justin recognized that.

I'm sure there are many advocates in the IL and broader disability community who think of Justin as a mentor. Certainly, there are others who were much closer to him than I was. All I can say is that Justin Dart had an immeasurable impact on my life. I wish I had told him that.

NCIL

The National Council on Independent Living (NCIL) is the consumer-controlled organization in Washington, D.C. that speaks on behalf of CILs, SILCs, and people with disabilities.

There are many other wonderful disability organizations out there--APRIL and SILC Congress among them, but none that invests both time and money to support independent living efforts like NCIL does.

Most of our legislative accomplishments, outcome measures, and operational actions occur because NCIL makes them priorities.

NCIL march

If you go to the NCIL Conference and it's your first time, make it a priority to go on the March to the Capitol--rain or shine.

I used to ask students in my classes to recall the first time they realized that they were part of a movement—that having a disability was not just an individual experience. You wouldn't believe how many people said it was the NCIL March to Capitol Hill.

There is something about being one of 500-plus people, many of whom are in wheelchairs, chanting and blocking traffic as they make their way toward the United States Capitol. I'll never forget rounding the corner onto Pennsylvania Avenue and seeing the Capitol for the first time amid that crowd.

Do yourself a favor. Go on the March. You won't regret it.

Some people never learn

Many years ago, centers for independent living (CILs) got so fed up with the Rehabilitation Services Administration (RSA) that they joined together and advocated for the elimination of RSA's regional offices. There was an office in each of 10 RSA geographic regions and the regional office staff was our primary contact with the feds.

Arizona was in RSA Region IX and our regional office was in San Francisco. I liked the woman who was our regional representative, but there were others in our region who found her hard to work with. This was often the case nationwide—a regional representative worked well with some states or agencies, but not with others. In at least three regions, the RSA regional representative was universally disliked.

As CILs pushed to eliminate these regional offices, the regulation establishing them came under fire.

When asked its opinion, NCIL acknowledged that many centers were frustrated by the unnecessary bureaucracy of the regional offices. NCIL took the side of those who wanted to eliminate them.

After the regional offices were closed, CILs discovered that people in the RSA central office in Washington, D.C. were just as rigid as the regional representatives had been.

So here we are today, trying to move out of RSA and into Health and Human Services because RSA refuse to listen to us and is unable to learn from their mistakes. For years, NCIL and others have complained to RSA about their position on a variety of issues that impact IL. Unfortunately, they chose to ignore us. Now they can't understand why we want to get out. Some people never learn.

Let's dance!

One of the great traditions in IL is the celebration held at the end of our conferences. Whether it's NCIL or APRIL or SILC Congress or some other gathering, time is set aside to get together and have a good time. The centerpiece of these parties is a dance.

As someone who has always loved to dance, I look forward to it. It's a time when people with disabilities can forget about being self-conscious and let loose like everyone else. Clearly, I'm not alone.

This year, because of my retirement, I will miss the NCIL Conference and its party. Have a beer and a dance for me!

Peer counseling

Peer counseling is a service that can only be provided by a person with a disability. It does not have to be provided by a person with the same type of disability as the consumer receiving the service.

Doing what comes naturally

I was the executive director of Liberty Resources, Inc. (LRI) from 1991-1995.

A couple of years after I left LRI, I had an opportunity to have lunch with an ex-employee of LRI and an LRI consumer. In the course of our dinner, this consumer told me a story that I will never forget.

Several years earlier, the consumer was sitting in the LRI lunchroom alone when I came in and joined her. She and I struck up a conversation and she told me about problems she was having at Temple University.

In the middle of class one day, she had the first of several epileptic seizures. After a brief hospitalization, the woman attempted to return to school. She continued to have seizures, which impeded her thought process and when she tried to speak to the professor about her situation, he was unsympathetic.

I encouraged her to stick it out, recommending that she start taping the lectures. More than anything, she recalled, I inspired her to hang in there.

The woman told me that this encouragement was exactly what she needed at the time. She went on to finish her Bachelor's degree and had started graduate school.

Truthfully, I don't remember the incident, but it goes to show you how much consumers look up to us. Whether you like it or not, all CIL employees are advocates, skills trainers, role models and counselors.

Is your center oppressing people?

Some time ago, I wrote a post on understanding the nature of oppression. In a nutshell, I said that all of us have been oppressed and that we need to get in touch with that oppression before we can overcome it. CILS can help this process and, if successful, can sometimes transform those who have been oppressed into committed advocates.

It would be terrible if centers were doing things that fed into the oppression people experience. How can we avoid doing that?

Remember that many of our consumers grew up under the Medical Model. You can remind consumers that a practitioner's educational accomplishments does not mean he or she knows more about the consumer than the consumer knows about himself or herself.

Consumers often received a substandard education and had horrible experiences in traditional classrooms. They have been relegated to the bottom rung on the ladder. They make the lowest wages, live in the poorest neighborhoods, and receive the worst health care.

Is your center feeding into consumer oppression? Are you overly concerned about your education? Are you stuck using traditional classroom methods? Do you take steps to make changes in your community or do you condone its substandard programs? Or something else?

Have you noticed that one of your peers is oppressing consumers? Do him or her a favor and share your concerns.

Speak up, damn it

I posted a short article encouraging consumers to speak up when they wanted something from a professional who is locked into the Medical Model.

Easy for me to say.

In reality, many consumers do not have the skills necessary to do this. They received a substandard education and were taught that these "professionals" knew more than they did about--well, everything.

Many people with disabilities have been so oppressed by society that they are unable to speak on their own behalf. As IL advocates, we can help consumers change, but it takes time. Until then, we look out for our brothers and sisters who are still learning. We're in this together.

Peer role modeling

Peers at centers for independent living (CILs) always have a disability. By law, you cannot provide peer counseling services at a CIL unless you have a disability. Every center must promote peer relationships and peer role modeling.

Beyond that, centers have a lot of latitude in determining how strong its peer programs will be. Some require that counselors have advanced degrees. Others have sophisticated volunteer programs that match consumers to role models in the community.

Most do something simpler. They have a staff member with a lot of common sense who provides one-on-one support, drawing on his or her own experience as a person with a disability.

When I was an executive director, I used to require that all staff members who had a disability serve as peer role models. They had to be people that were living or trying to live independently, so that consumers could emulate them. Simply put, if you had a disability and were also an employee of the center, you were expected to be a role model.

How did I implement this? We just did it. The law was clear enough that I didn't need to make any exceptions. If I were to do it today, I would make it a job requirement and have new employees sign a form acknowledging this expectation.

In 11 years as director, I only had one issue with this requirement. I had a staff member who was responsible for guiding consumers through a deinstitutionalization process, but the employee lived in a nursing home. We offered to help him transition to community housing and guaranteed that he would always have the support he needed. When he declined, we let him go.

I don't see how CILs can claim to be beacons of light for individuals who want to live independently and keep staff who do not have the same values. Whether it is a guy living in a nursing home or one who has lived too long with his parents, CILs need to be the one place where consumers are reinforced for thinking and acting independently.

Polio

I never really appreciated the fear that parents must have experienced during the polio outbreak of the forties and fifties. You never knew when or where it would strike. All you knew was that when it did strike, those affected would probably have severe breathing and gait problems for the rest of their lives.

Most people who got polio and are still living are in their 70's now. That means it's possible that someone new to the disability movement today has never met a person who experienced polio. Other than AIDS, no disease was more frightening.

I remember going to the neighborhood elementary school and standing in line to get a sugar cube that had been treated with the polio vaccine. That same scenario happened across the country and the treatment essentially wiped out the spread of the disease.

NPR recently did a segment on polio in Pakistan. Despite attempts to eradicate polio worldwide, there were 50 cases in northwest Pakistan last year. Much of the problem is related to the approach used by medical staff to reach children. The vaccination takes four separate inoculations, so parents are skeptical. Add to that rumors about what's in the vaccine, Taliban threats, and fears of foreign influence.

Believe me, we do not want another outbreak of polio.

Post-traumatic stress disorder (PTSD)

When I first started putting this guide together, I had everything related to PTSD under the Mental Health heading. However, because of my personal experience with PTSD, I found that several articles were exclusive to my own experience and belong in a separate section.

For those of you who do not know my history, I first experienced PTSD shortly after I returned from Vietnam. While there, I was involved in a massive rocket and mortar attack and got a concussion. I continued reliving that experience, waking up in the middle of the night and trying to figure out if I was dead or alive. The flashbacks, along with other symptoms continued for about five years and then went away.

When I was about 60, the PTSD symptoms returned. I was waking up in the middle of the night and could not go back to sleep. My road rage returned, my startle reflex could be triggered with the slightest noise, and I became paranoid when people stood directly behind me.

I recalled experiencing those symptoms when I first came home from Vietnam and immediately called the VA. They said that because I was a workaholic, I had successfully pushed aside negative symptoms while I worked and looked after my family. As I approached retirement, the anger and anxiety that I had suppressed for 40 years was coming to the surface.

The VA agreed that I have PTSD and possibly a traumatic brain injury (TBI) from the concussion.

Anger management

I took an Anger Management course to deal with problems I was having with Post-Traumatic Stress Disorder (PTSD). It was an excellent investment of my time.

One thing I learned is that people who have PTSD have disproportionate anger responses. While that is obvious to anyone who understands PTSD, it is not always apparent to others.

We all experience things that make us angry--heavy traffic, conversations with your ex, overbearing parents, etc. If we rated the level of anger related to one of these situations on a scale of 1 to 10, most of us would report it as 4 or 5.

A person who has PTSD is at a level 4 to 5 *all the time*, so when one of these situations occurs, the person with PTSD would rate it as an 8 or 9. If you encountered someone at an 8 or 9 walking down the street, you would probably cross the street to avoid that person.

When you take an anger management class, you're told that one of the best ways to elude these episodes is by avoiding the situations that trigger them altogether. This may seem obvious, and that's probably why it works. Staying off the highways during rush-hour and avoiding people who get on my nerves is the most effective way to deal with my condition.

Can meditation work for you?

Most of you do not know that I have Post-traumatic Stress Disorder (PTSD). My PTSD was result of being caught in a rocket and mortar attack in Vietnam. About five years ago, my symptoms of PTSD reappeared.

I could not sleep after 4 a.m. I started having serious road rage. I became startled every time there was a noise behind me. When I looked into it, I found that these symptoms had disappeared years ago when I became preoccupied with work. As I approached retirement though, many of the symptoms resurfaced. I discovered that over the years I had developed other habits that seemed insignificant but were ways to make having PTSD bearable.

One of the problems with losing sleep is that it impacts my other disability, affecting my balance and my speech. To make sure I get enough rest, I take medication that relaxes me and helps me sleep. I was finding however, that it was not enough.

Every morning, shortly before breakfast, I meditate for 20 minutes. I use a technique that I learned many years ago called "Transcendental Meditation," but there are many, many other forms of meditation that are readily available and easy to learn. Meditation reduces the amount of stress I feel first thing in the morning and throughout the day.

One of the things I am learning about PTSD is that it is not unique to veterans. Anyone who has experienced a life-threatening situation can experience these symptoms. I say "can" because everyone reacts differently. There are plenty of people who have gone through rocket and mortar attacks who do not get PTSD.

Meditation works for me. It might work for you, too.

Who should apologize?

One Friday night I attended an Arizona Diamondback's baseball game. I go to about 15 games a year and always take my wife or one of my two adult sons. This time, my 23-year-old went with me and I took my three-wheel scooter because there's a lot of walking involved.

Usually, before the game we have dinner at the Hard Rock Café across the street from the stadium. When we went into Hard Rock, we were given one of those vibrating/flashing alerts and told that it would be a 10 to 15 minute wait.

Several people who were behind me in line were seated ahead of us, and the wait became 30 minutes. Now, I understand that some of this seating might have been in an inaccessible area, but I was never consulted about my ability to get out of the chair. The manager approached me and asked me how things were going. I told him in no uncertain terms that the delay was unacceptable.

Instead of apologizing for the delay, he reprimanded me for using foul language in front of children in the waiting room. I really don't think the only "child" – a teenage girl -- was offended, but there is no excuse for bad language in front of families, whatever age.

So, who should apologize?

On one hand, should the manager try to address the needs of someone they felt was obnoxious? The manager doesn't know that in addition to my physical difficulties, I also have Post-Traumatic Stress Disorder (PTSD) and I got it serving in the military. He also doesn't know that there are many people, like me, who cannot control our anger once it has started.

For both of our sakes, I left after 45 minutes without being served.

I know I'm not the first customer with either of these disabilities to dine at a Hard Rock Café. I would expect that a business the size of the Hard Rock would be prepared to handle the flood of customers before a Friday game. They turned my pregame experience into a horror show.

Stop the train! I want to get off

I wrote a piece called "Guilt" about people who have PTSD and feel guilty about losing their friends. I never experienced guilt in this way, even though I had PTSD. Many people who have PTSD also experience increased anxiety on the anniversary of the incident that caused their PTSD. I don't experience that either.

People who have this disability experience a lot of different symptoms and respond to different forms of treatment. It seems like we're all unique, yet we have this common disability.

One of the symptoms that does appear to be common to people with PTSD is anger. Some of us control it better than others. As I wrote in a previous article ("Who Should Apologize?"), this has become a problem for me.

Once it starts, it feels like a runaway train and I'm unable to stop it.

One of the best steps I can take is to sidestep situations that are likely to set me off. I avoid traffic during rush hour and stay out of malls and shopping centers.

The best thing that someone can do for me when anger starts to arise is to take time to explain why a problem has occurred and what is being done to address it.

Responding to change

Change happens

CILs and SILCs still do things that do not make sense in light of changing dynamics in the field of Independent Living. Activities that made sense in the eighties do not make sense now.

Back then, we needed to gather medical evidence to prove consumers had disabilities and were eligible to receive services. We were also led to believe that nursing homes were a viable option for consumers. We thought "informed consent" meant telling parents of adult children with disabilities what we had up our sleeves. These were some of the obvious problems we tried to address when the Rehab Act was reauthorized in 1992.

There were other problems we created on our own. We placed the wrong people on our boards and in other positions of authority. We hired totally unqualified people to fill staff positions. Thirty years later, many of these same people are still affiliated with our centers and SILCs.

Of course we also have great people whose commitment and value to Independent Living is unquestioned.

We did not understand that staff must be role models, skills trainers should actually be able to train, and employees are expected to work regardless of their background.

If centers and SILCs pay employees a wage they do not earn, these organizations are no better than the sheltered workshops they criticize.

Scenarios

Early on, I found that students liked it when I used scenarios as part of the instruction. They often rated the use of scenarios as the best part of the training. I have included several scenarios that can also be found on my website. I have also included posts that address issues identified in those scenarios.

Using scenarios

These scenarios are meant to challenge your thinking. They ask you to make choices between the IL movement's philosophy, your own values, and real-world challenges.

The IL Philosophy is not intended to be placed on a pedestal without being challenged or questioned. It is alive and dynamic. The best CILs and SILCs discuss and debate our principles. They demand that our actions live up to our philosophy.

If you have an extra half-hour and four to eight friends to join in, set up your own small group session. Form a circle, give everyone a copy of the scenario, and have one participant read the scenario aloud. The group discusses the scenario and then someone reads the answers at the end. If you have more than one small group, add an extra 30 minutes for the group to come back together in one larger group to discuss and debate the respective answers.

There are a couple steps you can take to make processing these scenarios more meaningful. First, don't restrict yourself to your initial response. You will benefit from reacting to the views of others and they will gain insight from reacting to yours. The greatest benefit will be from the debate.

These scenarios work best if each of you feels free to comment on the responses of other participants. Be liberal with your kudos, constructively criticize, and offer supportive suggestions.

Scenario - board micromanagement

(If this is your first time using scenarios, you may wish to read the article "Using Scenarios" before getting started.)

This is a good scenario for boards of directors. Schedule 45 minutes before or after a board meeting to do this one.

Board Micromanagement

Jerry Baron was one of the founders of the Plaines Center for Independent Living (PCIL) and its first executive director. A series of nagging illnesses caused Jerry to miss so much work in his ninth year that he grudgingly resigned his position. It was clear to both Jerry and the board that the illness was likely to continue indefinitely and that Jerry could best serve the center in another capacity. They immediately appointed him to the board, where he is now serving as treasurer.

A new executive director, Sandy King, was hired three months later. Sandy had been the assistant director at the largest center in the state. Consumers, staff, and board members felt exceedingly lucky to bring Sandy on board. She was a woman with a disability who had started several excellent programs at her previous center, written their start-up grants, led the center's efforts at the Capitol, and supervised most of the staff.

Everything proceeded smoothly for 11 months when Sandy called Bill Guest and Maxine Caldwell, the chair and vice-chair of the board and asked for a meeting.

When they met, Sandy asked them about her performance. Each of them told her that they were pleased with her work. She had recently brought in funding to start two new programs, which meant hiring five additional staff. Plus, Sandy had convinced the local newspaper to feature two PCIL consumers who had moved out of nursing homes with their assistance. "I think I'm doing a good job, too." Sandy added.

As it turns out, Sandy had requested the meeting with the chairs so that she could complain about Jerry. It seems that he isn't satisfied with her performance. Jerry had been at the center the previous week, reviewing the salaries of the new positions and encouraging certain staff to compete for the jobs. Sandy was upset because these staff were woefully under-qualified and, "Jerry knows it," she claimed.

Jerry had also complained to these same staff that Sandy had undermined his pet recreational project, a turkey-shoot that only two consumers attended last year. When confronted by Sandy about both issues, Jerry responded that it was the treasurer's job to oversee salaries and look for program waste.

Sandy was fed up. "Look, either he goes or I go!" she demanded.

141

Bill looked to Maxine. "What can we do?" he moaned. "This is Jerry's center, so the rest of the board isn't going to offend him."

Questions:
1. Is this Jerry's center? If not, whose is it?
2. What mistakes did the board make that contributed to this problem?
3. What steps should the board take to address these issues?

Micromanagement

The two most common complaints I hear about boards of directors are that they are either not involved enough or too involved.

Boards that are "not involved enough" usually have problems with quorum and fundraising. This is a post about being too involved--or micromanaging.

Generally, micromanagement occurs for two reasons: 1) board members believe that they have been asked to micromanage, or 2) board members are afraid not to micromanage. In the first case, when a board member is recruited, he or she is asked to keep an eye on one or more staff members. Usually it's the bookkeeper who is providing (or supposed to be providing) monthly financial reports to the board.

The other reason board members micromanage is that they are afraid the organization will do something illegal or will mismanage funds in a way that draws IRS attention.

There are steps a center can take to reduce micromanagement. First, they can make sure everyone understands the line of authority. Most often, the key people are the executive director and the board chair. If all communication goes through these two individuals, a lot of miscommunication can be avoided.

Let's say that a board member hears a derogatory rumor about one of the staff. This board member should raise the issue to the board chair, who in turn will raise the issue to the executive director. A smart director will investigate the matter rapidly and report back to the board chair. The chair then decides whether it is appropriate to share the information with the board member who raised the concern.

Staff contribute to the problem when they discuss issues with board members. This usually occurs because the board member has a previous relationship with the staff member. Once a person joins the board, he or she needs to discontinue those kind of relationships with staff. If a staff member learns that he or she can bypass the executive director, the board member has essentially undermined leadership at the center.

Scenario: building coalitions

(If this is your first time using scenarios, you may wish to read the article "Using Scenarios" before getting started.)

Centers and SILCs run into this problem a lot. Is our involvement tacit approval?

Building Coalitions

Jim Johnson enjoyed the monthly meetings with other center directors. They were a fun group of people and the 10 of them had been meeting for almost three years. John especially liked that they were developing a strong coalition that was finally beginning to make some long-needed changes in the way the state agency dealt with centers.

Jim was chairing the group this year, so he jumped right into the first item on the agenda--joining the Disability Budget Coalition (DBC).

The DBC has a great reputation around the state. For $5,000 a year membership fee, an organization had access to DBC's library and capitol city offices, and most important, their lobbyist. The DBC lobbyist, Susan Flynn, was a tireless advocate for people with disabilities and a great communicator with both the membership and elected officials.

Jim, who put the item on the agenda, led off the discussion. "I know that $5,000 is more than most of us can afford, but the DBC has agreed to let us join as a group," he explained. "If all ten of us sign on, the DBC will let us join as a state association. That way the cost will be a manageable $500 each."

Bill Williams, who runs a center on the other side of the state, chimed in, "This will be great. We can finally begin to work on getting more money for centers and personal assistance services." The centers were confident that if they just had a presence at the capitol, they would be successful.

Susan had already assured them that she knew several legislators who consistently supported projects for people with disabilities. The centers would bring a much-needed consumer presence to the coalition. "This is a perfect match!" Bill added.

Mary Hathaway, who runs one of the few centers that can afford the $5,000, interrupted. "Shouldn't we think about who else belongs to the Coalition?" She went on to explain that another member was Goodwill Industries, which was pushing for funds to expand their sheltered workshop.

"Just because we work with DBC to get more funds for centers and PAS doesn't mean we need to advocate for sheltered workshops," Bill responded.

Questions:

1. Should the association join the DBC?
2. If no, why?
3. If yes, how do the centers deal with the sheltered workshop issue?

Sheltered workshops

Most of you have a pretty good idea what a sheltered workshop is. You most likely envision it as a facility for people with certain types of disabilities whose functioning levels are so low that they could never be successfully employed "in the real world." Consequently, we isolate them, pay them sub-minimum wages, and never train them to move into community employment.

What you probably do not realize is that an entire industry has evolved to address this "need." Sure, things have changed over the years. Sheltered workshops used to employ many people who were blind, and now they primarily employ people who are severely and profoundly retarded.

The quality of the work sheltered workshops offer also has improved somewhat. It used to be "pretend work" like separating nuts and bolts. (We used to joke that another sheltered workshop paid their employees to put them together in the evening.) Today, some companies contract with workshops to do menial, repetitive work and assume that the workers cherish these tasks.

Sheltered workshops have outlived their usefulness and need to be closed. Yet, government agencies continue to pay organizations to keep them going.

It's a sad statement about the education and training of people with disabilities in our society that sheltered employment exists. People with disabilities do not need archaic, segregated environments. They need real jobs with real wages.

Sheltered workshops stay open because operators of these workshops and their spokespeople perpetuate the idea that employment in segregated settings at sub-minimum wages is appropriate. They claim that there are 'certain' people with disabilities who will never be employable in the traditional sense and need this protected, artificial environment.

Unfortunately, the people who hold these outdated beliefs are the same professionals who are charged with training and educating this group. As any parent will tell you, if a teacher does not believe your child has the ability to learn, your child is probably not going to prove that teacher wrong.

Advocates of integrated work point out that operators of these sheltered workshops could, in fact, pay higher wages. They usually receive state funding for each worker, in addition to the compensation they get from contractors they do work for. Instead, they leverage the fear of family members who are happy with any program that looks after their family member to keep wages low.

If the "private and government entities" that are contracting with the sheltered workshops needed to look elsewhere for this work to be done, would they be able to bypass our minimum wage law? Maybe it's time to renegotiate their contracts and start giving these employees with disabilities a respectable wage.

Forty years ago, Marc Gold created a method for training people who were profoundly retarded called *Try Another Way*. Essentially, Marc (who has since passed away), felt that if we broke down tasks to their smallest steps, anybody could learn anything. Marc used to demonstrate this by teaching a profoundly retarded person he just met for the first time how to assemble a bicycle brake. His students became so adept at this that Bendix began hiring them.

The vast majority of people in the disability community are employable and eager to work. By allowing sheltered work to continue, society perpetuates the negative and false stereotype that people with disabilities are less capable than everyone else.

When we discover segregated facilities in third-world countries where the workers earn a pittance and have no hope of advancement, we call them sweatshops. Why do we have a lower standard for our own citizens?

We need to give everyone pay that is commensurate with what they do and offer them work in an integrated environment. Of course there are people who lack the skills necessary to compete in the competitive workforce, and we should be ashamed of enabling a system that continues producing them.

The people who run sheltered workshops aren't bad people and neither are the family members who desperately want six hours of supervised care during the day. Let's just stop pretending that this is real work.

Sheltered employment is to workforce development what shock therapy is to mental health treatment.

If you want to see how Marc's program works, watch the video at Try Another Way.

Scenario - conflicting interests

(If this is your first experience with scenarios, you may wish to read "Using Scenarios" before getting started.)

Is a staff member only an employee from 8-5? If not, how much jurisdiction does the center have over after-hours activities?

The following is a scenario about staff commitment to our philosophy.

Conflicting Interests

Jim Forester is the executive director of the Eastlake Center for Independence (ECI).

Last month, the board of directors of ECI met for two days and constructed a three-year strategic plan. A lengthy discussion arose about the notorious state-run institution for people with developmental disabilities (DD) called the Eastlake Training Program (ETP) that is located on the outskirts of town.

The closure of the state facility had been in process for some time, but encountered resistance from employees who would lose their jobs at the institution. In addition to the concerns about employment, workers in the institutions and their families were scaring people in the community with negative stories about people with developmental disabilities.

The board of directors agreed during their strategic planning session, by a narrow 6-5 vote, to join efforts to close the facility. Jim was directed by the board chair to immediately start working with the state to "do whatever we can to help."

Jim shared the plan with the staff and specifically told them about the center's position on the closure of the institution. The head of the state's DD program welcomed their involvement when he heard about the center's new commitment. In spite of developing a wide array of community-based residences and opportunities for employment, the community was still resisting closure.

Jim and his staff thought the greatest contribution that they could make would be to address the misperceptions that the community had about people with developmental disabilities. The center's strategy involved making a series of presentations in the community geared to educating their citizens about this segment of the disability population. The center also purchased several videos that could be shown to support their presentations.

After six months, there was still considerable resistance to the closure. Although the presentations received a positive response, broad opposition from employees, their families, and the union that represented them continued.

One evening, on the local CBS station, there was coverage of a rally against closing the institution. Standing directly behind the main speaker and holding a sign that said "Keep ETP Open" was Marcia Robins, a staff member from the center.

At 8:00 a.m. the next day, the board chair was on the phone. "Jim, you need to fire Marcia immediately," the chair directed. When Jim expressed concern that the center did not have a policy on after-hour activities, the chair said, "I don't care. She knows the center's position."

Questions

1. Is it important that the staff support the center's position?
2. How should Jim handle this problem?
3. How could this predicament have been avoided?

Scenario: hard choices

(If this is your first time using scenarios, you may wish to read the previous article on "Using Scenarios.")

By the way, the best scenarios are the ones where you find yourself arguing from one side while your colleagues argue from the other. Welcome to Hard Choices.

Hard Choices

Fran Luce is a 22-year old consumer of the Central State Center for Independent Living (CSCIL), a center in a small rural community. She has become one of the center's "stars," moving out on her own, getting a job, and then enrolling in a college located in the next town. CSCIL had helped her find a personal assistant, modified her apartment, and given her moral support as she overcame the barriers she faced in their community.

Recently, she came into the center crying. Apparently, she was pregnant. Marriage was not an option, and if she decided to have the baby she would need to drop out of school and give up her apartment. Fran was looking for a quick solution to her problem and wanted the staff's assistance in arranging an abortion.

Jane Barkley, the IL specialist who worked most with Fran, was equally distressed. She was adamantly opposed to abortion and was alarmed that Fran refused to even discuss other options. Unable to come up with alternatives, Jane decided to refer Fran to the Planned Parenthood office near the college. However, because she was uncomfortable, Jane thought she better run her decision by the executive director, Bill Fraley.

"Are you serious?" he asked. "There isn't a single member of our board who would support a referral to Planned Parenthood. In fact, there aren't more than a handful of people in this whole town who would support it."

Bill was right, of course. This little church-oriented community had successfully passed ordinances outlawing alcohol sales and gambling. If the community became aware of a referral to Planned Parenthood, all support for the center would cease immediately.

Discussion questions:

1. What should Jane do?

2. How seriously should community preferences be taken?

3. What direction should Bill give to Jane?

What would you do?

One of the toughest IL concepts to understand is related to "choice." Many advocates believe that once a consumer makes a choice, centers are required to help him or her carry out their decision.

I don't agree.

Just because a consumer makes a decision does not mean we must help him or her carry it out. For some reason, otherwise clear-thinking advocates believe that because a consumer makes a choice we have to abide by that decision, even if it violates IL philosophy.

There is a difference between respecting someone's right to make a choice and helping that person fulfill it. In one of my trainings I have a scenario in which a consumer, after reviewing all of the options, chooses to go into a nursing home. The dilemma is whether or not CIL staff should assist him. I say no! Centers never support institutionalization. Most people in my trainings disagree with me and do not see this as a violation of our principles.

My best example is a scenario in which a pregnant woman goes into Catholic Community Services (CCS) and tells them she would like an abortion.

The CCS staff would talk to her about adoption, in-home supports, foster care, and other options. At the end of their discussion, if the woman still wants an abortion are they going to send her to a clinic? Of course not!

Helping someone get an abortion is inconsistent with CCS's philosophy. No one would question their refusal to help, yet here we are saying that a center should institutionalize someone because they request it.

What do you think?

Tug of war

What happens when a center for independent living (CIL) wants to go in a direction that is counter to the values of its community?

We like to think we are community-based, but we all know that communities can be really slow to make the changes necessary for us to live independently. So, what do we do? How hard do we push for change?

Making this decision fits within the board's role. They should have a good sense of what the community will tolerate and the capabilities of their CIL. If there is healthy communication between the staff (through the ED) and board, center leadership will understand the issues, steps already taken to address them, and additional action needed.

When planning Board meetings, provide enough time in the agenda to debate issues. Do not be afraid to discuss the most radical approaches--or to walk away from bad ideas.

Boards should have members with a wide range of perspectives. If your board never wants to try anything new or always defends the status quo, it's probably time to change members.

The best centers and SILCs are the ones that discuss and debate issues and stand behind their principles.

Scenario: Hug this

(If this is your first time using scenarios, you may wish to read the previous article on "Using Scenarios.")

Here is a dilemma that many centers face--commitments that conflict with your principles.

Hug this

Westcore Center for Independent Living (WCIL) has been trying to create a new image for itself in the community. In the past, the center had worked primarily with consumers with developmental disabilities, offering a variety of day care and recreational activities.

Earlier this year the board hired a new executive director, John Ford, and asked him to begin exploring new ways to reach out to other disability populations. A review of the center's demographics showed that almost all other disability groups were under-represented, especially consumers in the 22 to 35 age range.

John began integrating a variety of new social and recreational programs into the center's services. They formed a quad rugby team and began holding more social activities in popular meeting places in the community. The center also added some energetic peer role models to the staff, and liberalized their transportation program to give consumers more freedom to attend unsupervised adult activities.

In the end, however, these efforts were only moderately successful. John was dumbfounded and shared his concerns with the staff.

"I don't know why you're surprised," said Brian Thomas. "Everybody in the community thinks we're nothing but a DD program, and as long as we continue to take such a large role in Special Olympics that image will never change."

WCIL expends a lot of resources on Special Olympics, recruiting volunteers and working the events. In addition, their largest fund raising activity is an awards banquet following Special Olympics. The annual event is hosted by their board of directors, with the current President as the master of ceremonies. Last year's banquet raised $50,000.

"He's right," Connie Sparks chimed in, "a center shouldn't even support a segregated, demeaning event like the Special Olympics, and as long as we do, these other consumers will stay away."

Questions:
1. Are Brian and Connie right?
2. How should John handle this? Should he talk to the board? If so, what does he say?

Scenario: Starting from scratch

(If this is your first time using scenarios, you may wish to read the previous article on "Using Scenarios.")

I began constructing this scenario in 2000-2001 as part of a board of directors' training I was developing. The training was designed to force participants to look at their center from the bottom up, and to look closely at what works and what does not. The trick in developing this scenario was wiping out the center without killing everyone. I actually considered calling the scenario "Ground Zero." Then 9/11 happened.

The following scenario is intended to allow you to think outside the box. I say "allow" because I suspect that several of you will want to replicate your current program. If you are in a group, look around. Some of your peers are probably biting their tongues.

Starting from Scratch

Last night your center and half of the town were wiped out by a hurricane. You have nothing except the piece of land upon which your center used to stand. Your six staff members are safe, but each has called to tell you that he or she is not coming back. One will be taking an early retirement, three are moving out of town, and two are moving in with their parents to help them rebuild their homes.

This morning you spoke at length with representatives from RSA, which holds your center's Part C grant. You have called an emergency board meeting at your home, realizing that many of the 12 members may not be able to attend. You are surprised when eight show up, including the President and Treasurer.

It's clear to you that this has to be a short, down-to-business meeting, so you jump right in. "I just spent an hour with the Commissioner of RSA, her deputy, and the Chief of the Independent Living Unit. They are being incredibly supportive," you tell your board.

You go on to inform them that your $300,000 Part C grant is just starting and RSA agreed to continue it as long as center operations keep developing. RSA informed you that they would like a brief report in six months outlining your progress.

"That's great," your board president exclaimed, "with the insurance money, we'll be back on our feet in no time at all!"

"Wait a minute," the Treasurer chimed in, "let's turn this problem into an opportunity and create a whole new center."

Truthfully, you and the board have had lengthy discussions lately about services and operations at the center. Although the center was running satisfactorily, it was plodding along.
Maybe the Treasurer is right. It is time to start thinking outside the box.

Questions:
1. If this was YOUR center, what would you propose for your core services?
2. How would you change your job at the center if you had to completely re-create it?

Scenario - Taking risks

(If this is your first time using scenarios, you may wish to read the previous article on "Using Scenarios.")

This is a scenario that I developed to enhance my *Discovering the Leaders Among Us* training on grassroots leadership development.

Taking Risks

You are the director of a center for independent living. When you got to work today, there were two consumers waiting to see you. You can tell that they are upset and concerned about something, so you postpone a meeting with one of your staff so that you can see them immediately.

As soon as you are alone with them, the consumers begin complaining that the center has "lost its way." They feel that the center, in order to become financially secure, has become too service-oriented and too concerned with "making the state happy."

You agree with them and tell them so. You explain about the need for fund raising and making payroll, and talk about the pressure from your board chair to "put on a good face in the community" and increase contributions by 25 percent in the next year. What you don't tell them is that the board chair probably hasn't read the mission statement since it was written three years ago.

One of the consumers points out that the board was precisely the problem, and that one way to get on track was to add true consumers to the board. The consumers knew that there was an opening on the board, since one of the center founders had recently passed away. At that point, the consumers said what was on their mind from the beginning of the meeting -- they recommended that the center add Frank Donavan to the board.

You try to hide your initial reaction.

Frank is very controversial. He founded an organization called *Crip Power!* five years ago and his name has become synonymous with angry, hard-hitting, in-your-face advocacy. Frank almost single-handedly forced the city to make its offices and recreational facilities accessible and literally halted vans on the street that did not have working lifts. Recently, while being arrested, Frank told a local television station that the mayor was a "fascist pig" and threatened to "blow up" City Hall.

Crip Power! has never really gotten off the ground. Although the organization has several members, Frank lacks the skills to set out an organizational plan of action and follow it.

On the plus side, you always know exactly what is on Frank's mind. He would give you an honest, straight-forward opinion and would keep the board on track with regard to the center's mission. What Frank lacks in organizational management skill, he makes up in passion. His addition to the board would send a strong, positive message to the disability community. The other board members would either love him or hate him.

The board has traditionally followed your recommendation regarding new members and you suspect that they will this time as well. Your heart says to put his name forward. Your brain says to back away.

Questions:

1. Do you take the risk?
2. Who does the executive director work for?

Who's in charge?

As some of you know, I used to run the center in Philadelphia. The center in Philadelphia wasn't then, and isn't now, a typical CIL.

We always viewed ourselves, first and foremost, as an advocacy agency. We were also a very good service provider, so the state entrusted us with lucrative personal assistance and deinstitutionalization programs. When the state was mad at us, we became even stronger because we had a loyal consumer base that continued to use our programs.

While I was there, we began adding consumers to our board of directors. Now, I'm not talking about professionals who happen to have disabilities. These were people who had moved to the community after living for 12 and 24 years in a nursing home. Talk about changing the dynamics of board meetings!

In addition to this change, the center and its consumers took on the city, state, and federal government in a series of lawsuits. At one time, we were suing the state twice because they failed to implement the Motor Voter Law and because they failed to pull down federal funds available for deinstitutionalization. This came on top of the Third Circuit decision against the City of Philadelphia regarding curb cuts and prior to our work on Helen L., the precursor to Olmstead.

I'm telling you all of this to give you some sense of the climate at this center.

The board of directors had several members, including officers, who had joined the board around the time I first came to the center. They weren't comfortable with the changes that were happening, but seemed to go along with the movement.

Not long after I left in 1995, they needed to add a new member to the board and these board members made a unilateral decision to nominate a man who was in a high-up position at local nursing home. This nursing home called itself a rehab center, but in fact was the place where a lot of younger folks were warehoused after acquiring a disability.

The staff and consumers were flabbergasted. Whether this man was qualified or not, I don't know. The consumers and staff just saw this as further example of how out-of-touch these board members were.

On the night of the board meeting, a large number of consumers took over the room and stopped the meeting, demanding the resignations of these board members. As I understand it, most of them resigned that evening.

This center continues to this day to be one of the strongest in the country, and there is no doubt about who is in charge.

How did it happen?

I wrote a post called *Who's in Charge and* received several comments about the posting from readers who complained that consumers taking over a board meeting could never happen at their center.

That may or may not be true, but let me tell you about the environment I entered.

First of all, the previous director had actually told the staff that they were not allowed to do advocacy, even though it is one of the four core services. I would never have believed this if I hadn't personally observed it, and seen it *in writing*.

To the board's credit, they put the more open-minded members in charge of recruitment and hiring the new ED. Many in the disability community were upset with the center, but didn't know where to turn. I was hired because of my firm commitment to advocacy.

We took several steps to change the Center's direction. First, we started a group called "Consumer Connection" that was coordinated by a staff member but run entirely by consumers. In addition, I re-hired a center employee who was a strong advocate and who had been forced out by the previous director.

These were only superficial changes. The rest of it had to do with attitude. My supervisory staff and I took every action we could think of to support strong advocacy.

Staff were not invited to participate in Consumer Connection. There were several times when I passed the room and consumers were adamantly voicing their concerns to elected officials.

Every time an event was hosted by American Disabled for Attendant Programs Today (ADAPT) I covered the staff advocate's costs to attend. It didn't take long before other staff started asking to go as well.

I used IL Skills Training funds to pay for advocacy training, which was then used to support ADAPT demonstrations. We gave staff time off to attend demonstrations if they used it as a training platform for consumers. We looked the other way when staff were arrested while demonstrating for the rights of people with disabilities.

We added consumers (<u>real</u> consumers) to our board of directors. We used core service funds to send a staff member to Washington, D.C. to advocate for healthcare for people with disabilities. We found a way to use personal assistance funds to support consumers who were advocating in Harrisburg or Washington, D.C.

160

These are just a few steps that can be taken to support advocacy in a center. These efforts demonstrated to advocates that we were behind their efforts. When advocates in the community knew they had our support, their work took on a life of its own.

Scenario - You call this work?

(If this is your first time using scenarios, you may wish to read the previous article on "Using Scenarios.")

You Call This Work?

Claudia Torres has been a member of the statewide independent living council (SILC) for four years and is currently serving as Chair of the Public Policy Committee. One of the major issues confronting people with disabilities is the Department of Vocational Rehabilitation's (DVR) over-reliance on sheltered workshops as an employment setting for persons in their community. Claudia and other members of the council feel that precious funds are being wasted in segregated settings when they could be used to develop integrated jobs in the business community. To make matters worse, many of the sheltered workshops are paying their workers less than the minimum wage.

Claudia and several members of her committee had five meetings with the workshop directors and the head of DVR in an effort to get funds redirected toward integrated programs in the community. On each occasion, suggestions put forward by the committee were rejected by the directors, who expressed concern about the feelings of their boards and the parents of their employees. "Besides," they responded, "these people just couldn't make it in real jobs."

The DVR director understood the Council's concern, but was not inclined to reverse 30 years of support given to the workshops.

Claudia and her committee met at the entrance to one of the workshops, Goodwill Industries. Several local activists were blocking the front of the building to protest the continued funding of Goodwill's segregated workshop, and Claudia was attending to show her support. When she arrived, several parents were arguing loudly with the activists and staff of the local center for independent living (CIL).

Claudia was pleased to see the CIL staff. The CIL director was on the SILC and always supported their advocacy efforts. As she arrived, Claudia saw that one of the center staff was being interviewed by the local TV station.

At the same time, however, another van – one from the CIL – pulled up and dropped off a consumer who was an employee at the sheltered workshop. The TV crew ignored the obvious contradiction, but Claudia did not. "How could you bring one of your consumers to this sheltered workshop!" she shouted. "What in the world do you stand for?"

Embarrassed, the CIL staff member replied, "But it's her choice. She wants to come here."

Questions:
1. Is the center right to transport a consumer to a segregated setting?
2. How might a peer counselor work with this consumer?
3. Does the board have any responsibility here?

Skills training

When centers first started in the 1980s, it was the dream of every CIL to create an accessible kitchen to teach consumers who wished to move into the community how to cook for themselves.

It didn't take centers long to realize that most apartments in the community are not accessible and that consumers just wanted to learn how to prepare food using a microwave. We have become smarter over the years and understand that adults learn differently than children and everybody has different learning goals.

What is your learning style?

When I used to teach Standards and Indicators, I included the Barsch/Haynie Learning Style Inventory (LS I) in my module on IL Skills Training. The LSI is a self-administered tool that helps people understand how they learn.

Normally, I would post a copy of the LSI in Bob's Tool Box. Unfortunately, while I can use the inventory in a classroom setting, posting it on the Internet would be a copyright violation.

The developers of the LSI say that people are either visual, auditory, or tactile learners. Those who complete this inventory gain a better understanding of how they absorb information.

My reason for sharing the LSI was to show trainers that students in their classes learn in different ways. There is a tendency on the part of new trainers to assume that everyone learns the same way. Not true. After all, that is not the way **we** learn. Yet, centers continue to purchase canned training modules and assume they apply to everyone.

Benefits counseling

There is a segment of the disability community that believes CILs should never provide Benefits Counseling. They believe that providing this service sends a message to consumers that reliance on government handouts is acceptable.

On the other hand, IL communities are learning that there are a number of services available to consumers that would benefit them but are not being used.

The challenge is how to provide access to needed services and benefits without promoting a reliance on them.

IL skills training

When it comes to the provision of IL Skills Training, CILs have come a long way. Since most of our consumers are not children, we have learned that they don't start with a blank slate.

For example, many consumers have a strong negative reaction to traditional classroom instruction. And we have learned that it makes no sense to train someone to use a fully accessible kitchen unless they have one at home.

I remember watching a staff member with a c-6 spinal cord injury teach a newly-disabled man with a similar disability how to pick a pencil up off the floor. This training took place in our lobby and was done in about five minutes.

The first person we moved out of a nursing home and into an apartment had Guillain-Barre Syndrome. One of our staff stayed with him and his attendant during his first dinner. Imagine our surprise when our consumer ate like he was at a trough. Although he had some use of his arms and hands, he had not fed himself for years because the nursing home had decided it took too much time. With very little training (mostly knowing when NOT to help), this man was eating on his own within the week.

In both of these incidents, we did very little "training" – that's what makes centers special.

Don't get caught up in the need to do formal training. This is the kind of activity that really makes a difference.

Here are some principles of adult learning. I don't remember where I found them, but they are good food for thought.

Principles of Adult Learning

"Treat learners like adults"

1. Adults are people with years of experience and a wealth of knowledge.
2. Adults have established values, beliefs and opinions.
3. Adults' style and pace of learning changes over time.
4. Adults relate new knowledge and information to their existing knowledge and previous experience.
5. Adult bodies are influenced by gravity.
6. Adults have pride.
7. Adults have a deep need to be self-directed.
8. Individual differences among people increase with age.
9. Adults tend to have a problem-centered orientation to learning.

Staff fund raising

Losing track

Theoretically, fund raising is the responsibility of the board of directors. In CILs, the majority of board members must be people with disabilities. The sad truth is that most people with disabilities are not in the upper levels of business or corporations. They can't trade favors with other corporate officers to assure their pet projects get funded.

As a result, fund raising often falls on the staff. Sometimes a board member will take the lead on an event, with staff doing much of the hard work. Regardless of who takes the lead, someone needs to be sure that the center does not lose track of its principles and philosophy in its efforts to raise funds.

Usually, no single incident or issue violates IL principles so strongly that it prevents CIL participation. For instance, holding an event at a facility that is inaccessible 23 years after the ADA became law is something that would cross the line. More likely, you make gradual concessions until you find yourself promoting something that is inconsistent with IL Philosophy.

Before you hold an event, determine what the center's position is on certain practices. For instance, should the center hold events under the following conditions?

- Some people cannot participate because of their disability, for example a 10k or road rally.
- Participation by some people may be harmful, such as wine tasting.
- Many consumers cannot participate because the event is expensive.
- Disability stereotypes may be perpetuated, for example bingo and Special Olympics.
- Corporations sponsoring the event manufacture products that are harmful, such as cigarettes or firearms.
- The event includes participation or sponsorship by corporations with employment practices that are detrimental to employees with disabilities, such as reducing employee hours to bypass health care obligations.
- The event includes organizations that take positions counter to IL Philosophy, such as advocating to keep institutions open due to staff layoffs.
- Inaccurate or off-putting images used to garner sympathy, such as the MDA telethon.

I'm not saying that any of these are right or wrong, but centers need to go into fund raising with their eyes wide open.

Who should speak up? Anyone. Everyone. If you believe that your center has crossed a line -- say so. The worst thing we can do is lose track of who we are.

Statewide Independent Living Council (SILC)

SILCs are an important part of the independent living movement. They represent an attempt to place genuine authority for state independent living programs in the hands of people with disabilities.

SILCs: Why we need them

When the idea of a statewide independent living council (SILC) first came up in 1992, advocates had both misgivings and high hopes. They were worried because the predecessors to SILCs had been created as advisory councils and answered to the state's vocational rehabilitation agency. Advocates were concerned that decision-making authority of the SILC would remain with VR.

Their concerns were justified. Many governors don't seem to respect the SILC and appoint unqualified people or give a low priority to appointing members. VR agencies are still reluctant to give up their authority 20 years later. SILC members are confused about their role and frequently advocate for self-serving and short-sighted expenditures. To make matters worse, the feds in D.C. have given a very narrow interpretation to the duties of the SILC.

On the other hand, SILCs are consumer controlled. In 1992, they were given authority to make decisions about the IL network in the state. For the first time, IL funds may be controlled by people with disabilities. I say "may" because many SILCs still give in to state agencies and are not assuring that community needs are given the highest priority, in spite of the legal backing to do so.

SILCs need to assert their rights. What are people with disabilities in the state saying they need? Both the law and the regulations require that the "State plan must provide for...**the needs in the State for...**" IL services.

The SILC is not an arm of the CIL nor a tool of the designated state unit (DSU). If SILC members take time to understand their role and try to fulfill it, they will play a meaningful role in creating changes that benefit people with disabilities in their state. Plus, it would be one more step the disability community takes to be in charge of the programs that affect them.

Why you should join a SILC

The independent living movement is squandering its best minds by not encouraging strong advocates to serve on statewide independent living councils (SILCs). There are great leaders out there who are not contributing their considerable skills to the cause.

I have always strongly supported SILCs. For the first time, we have an organization comprised of a majority of people with disabilities deciding how IL funds are spent. They decide how federal funds are spent and what the IL network will look like.

There are some DSUs and CILs that do not want to share responsibility for the IL network with SILCs. Those organizations need to understand that services to people with disabilities in the state are not limited to vocational rehabilitation and center programs. If we ever want to become independent in our communities, advocates need to move beyond the status quo.

Are SILCs frustrated by those who are afraid of change? Sure. But until we take an active role in directing our future, others will be glad to make decisions for us.

If you have time to spare, contact your SILC office, but don't volunteer unless you're planning to work.

If you live in an outlying area, don't let travel scare you off. SILCs will be happy to accommodate you.

Composition of the SILC

In 1992 when the composition of the SILC was being defined, it never occurred to us that people who didn't know anything about IL would try to get appointed to a SILC. The only safeguard in the law was that applicants had to be "knowledgeable" about CILs and IL services.

What does it mean to be knowledgeable about CILs and IL services? That you know they exist, or that you embrace the principles and philosophy behind them? If the latter was the requirement, how many of our DSU directors with their staunch commitment to the medical model would qualify?

Everyone who is appointed to the SILC should get an IL refresher and visit the centers in their state. You cannot do your job if you don't understand how the system works.

Here are some facts you should know about the composition of the SILC:

1. The majority of the members must be people with disabilities, excluding those members who are <u>employees</u> of state agencies and CILs, regardless of whether they are representing that agency or not.
2. CIL employees are allowed to vote.
3. State employees who are <u>NOT</u> representing state agencies are allowed to vote.
4. Employees representing state agencies are not allowed to vote.
5. The person representing the 121 program, if there is one, is allowed to vote.

If you want to know more about the composition of the SILC, go to:
http://www.ilru.org/section-53-appointment-and-composition

Appointments to the SILC

The Rehab Act states that the governor of each state must make the appointments to the SILC. An exception to the governor's appointment rule can be made if the SILC is placed in another organization, such as the state Board of Education. This situation only exists in one or two states, and in those states, the organization in which the SILC is placed has appointing authority.

These are some facts you should know about appointments:

1. Every member must be appointed, even those who are on the SILC because of the job they hold.
2. People whose terms expire are no longer members.
3. A state law that permits members to stay on other Councils until they are replaced or reappointed does not apply to SILCs.

People who are appointed on behalf of the state agency and the 121 programs are representatives subject to term limits and do not have to be the directors.

The Governor may delegate the authority to fill a vacancy to the remaining voting members of the Council after initial appointments expire or are vacated.

If you want to know more about SILC appointments, go to: http://www.ilru.org/section-53-appointment-and-composition.

How SILC Congress got started

In the late nineties, several of us from the National Council on Independent Living (NCIL) met with Judy Heumann, head of the Office of Special Education and Rehabilitative Services, to discuss changes we would like to see in the Rehab Act. When we suggested strengthening the statewide independent living councils (SILCs), she shared some negative comments she had heard about the SILCs. She had been told that several SILCs were operating as puppets of the Designated State Unit (DSU) and were preserving the system we worked so hard to replace.

Shortly after that meeting, Independent Living Research Utilization (ILRU) put on a SILC training in Milwaukee. During the training, I shared Judy's concerns, and those attending the training asked that ILRU host a conference of all of the SILCs. The SILC members attending the training told me that they wanted the conference to be in January, before legislatures were in session. They wanted this training to include a discussion of the primary issues facing SILCs.

When I got home, I immediately called my contact at ILRU, Laurel Richards. I shared what the SILCs had requested and we agreed to hold the conference in Houston, and that ILRU staff would serve as the conference planners. ILRU covered the cost of lodging and conference rooms and each state could send two SILC representatives.

Laurel and I discussed what an appropriate name for the conference would be. While talking with her, I did a word search on my computer. Eventually "Congress" appeared and we settled on that.

In order to come up with a list of primary issues, we conducted a survey. We asked each SILC to send us a list of their primary concerns/issues. We consolidated these responses into one common list and then asked SILCs to identify priorities from this common list.

Their top four issues were:
- The SILC relationship with the DSU
- The SILC relationship with centers for independent living
- SILC autonomy
- The SILC as a systems advocate

We concentrated on these areas during the conference and brought in four individuals to facilitate discussion and oversee the reporting out process. Those four individuals were Quentin Smith, Gina McDonald, Duane French, and me.

The first SILC Congress (held in January 1998) was a rousing success! Every state was represented and all agreed that the conference was productive and worthwhile.

In the second year, the Texas SILC did not send a representative. The participants asked that ILRU continue to support the Congress, but be held in a different state. The next year it was held in California.

Although several NCIL leaders were also members and directors of SILCs, NCIL was not formally involved for several years. Many SILC representatives felt that SILC Congress should be a separate entity. Eventually, NCIL began offering memberships to the SILC in each state.

Suicide

Suicide Prevention

The recent death of Robin Williams has led to many discussions about suicide. Let's not forget the implications for a center.

Often, centers come across consumers who are grappling unsuccessfully with the challenges that they face. In other words, our consumers are like everyone else.

The first thing we can do to address this issue is recognize when suicide may be a problem. Here are 10 warning signs that I got from Suicide Awareness Voices of Education (SAVE):

- Talking about suicide. Is the person talking about suicide, dying, or self-harm?
- Seeking out lethal means. Is the person seeking guns, pills, knives, or other objects that could be used in a suicide attempt?
- Preoccupation with death. Is there an unusual focus on death, dying, or violence?
- No hope for the future. Are there feelings of helplessness, hopelessness, and being trapped?
- Self-loathing/self-hatred. Are there feelings of worthlessness, guilt, shame, and self-hatred?
- Getting affairs in order. Is a person making out a will, giving away prized possessions, and/or making arrangements for family members?
- Saying goodbye. Are there unusual or unexpected visits or calls to families and friends?
- Withdrawn from others. Is the person with strong friends and family keeping to themselves?
- Self-destructive behavior. Is there an increased alcohol or drug use, reckless driving, unsafe sex, or acting as if they have a death wish?
- Sudden sense of calm. Is there a sudden sense of calm and happiness after being extremely depressed?

These are only warning signs. For more information about what you actually do if you see one or more of these signs, go to
http://www.helpguide.org/mental/suicide_prevention.htm

The competence-deviance hypothesis

Earlier this year I posted a criticism of sheltered employment. As part of that article, I discussed the work of Marc Gold, who had developed a method of training called "Try Another Way." Essentially, Marc disproved many of the ideas we have about the ability of developmentally disabled adults to learn and perform complex tasks.

One of the skills Marc taught his students was to put together bicycle brakes. Assembling a brake is a complex task and, although somewhat slower than their peers, the trainees' made fewer assembly errors. Consequently, companies like Bendix hired Marc's graduates.

Shortly thereafter, the non-disabled employees began to complain about their disabled peers. Apparently, the non-disabled employees felt that the personal hygiene of one of the disabled folks was too offensive to tolerate.

Rather than let a valued employee go, however, the company built a barrier around the work site of the offending employee, which reduced visual and olfactory contact with his peers.

After this experience, Dr. Gold formulated the competence-deviance hypothesis. The premise is that the more competent an individual is, the more deviance will be tolerated in him or her by others.

Two thoughts on this...

Not everyone can, or wants to, assemble bicycle brakes. Whether you are a bagger at the grocery store or a detailer at a car wash, or a lawyer at a law firm, employers want employees who show up on time and work hard.

One of the most valuable skills we can teach our consumers is personal care. If we really want our consumers to compete in the workforce, we need to be honest with them. Segregation is never a viable option.

The fog index

Every once in a while, a document crosses my desk and I find myself re-reading it. Thinking there must be a grammatical error, I re-read it again. Then I realize that it is not an error in grammar, the document was just written for someone a lot smarter than I (or is it *me*?).

When this happens, I pull out my Fog Index. The Fog Index is a handy tool that measures readability of the language used in a document. The index estimates the years of education needed to understand the text. A fog index of 12 requires the reading level of a U.S. high school senior (around 18 years old). The test was developed in 1952 by Robert Gunning, a professor at UCLA. The Index is widely available on the Internet.

The Fog Index is used to determine how well a document intended to explain something to a specific audience is likely to be understood by them. When writing for the general public, a document needs to have an index below 8. Centers and SILCs that are about to pay to have a brochure produced may want to apply the Fog Index. It would be a shame to pay for something that you need a Ph.D. to understand.

By the way, the Fox Index for the second paragraph above is 9.2.

Training staff

Every time there is a budget shortfall in this state and most others, the legislature cuts back funding for education. We rightfully complain that legislators are being short-sighted by not investing in our future. Why would anybody give education a low priority?

Yet, we do the same thing at centers. What are the first expenses we cut? Library, then travel. If you're like most CILs, you've been through so many cuts you don't even remember having a library.

There aren't many studies that show the return on investment for businesses who train their staff. We do know that when staff receiving proper training, there is less staff turnover, greater productivity, higher consumer satisfaction, and a decreased need to monitor and guide employees.

One of my favorite sayings is: "The only thing worse than training staff and having them leave, is not training them and having them stay."

I don't expect that our funders are going to be as enlightened as we are about training, but if you can't get around reducing your training budget, don't forget that there are lots of really good, cost-effective training options out there.

Trapped customers

Remember what it was like at the Post Office before Fed Ex and UPS? How about the DMV? Something seems to happen to employees whose customers have nowhere else to go to receive a service.

A friend of mine who used to do Total Quality Management (TQM) training called customers with only one service option "trapped customers."

Organizations that have trapped customers have a tendency to take these customers for granted. They treat them with less respect than others and rely on policies and procedures that are needlessly bureaucratic. Not surprisingly, customers become resentful.

If your center has consumers who are forced to get certain services from you, make sure you are treating them with respect. It doesn't cost anything to be nice.

Traps and Pitfalls

Sometimes a center loses track of what made it special.

Maybe the funding source never really understood IL, or a staff member who was not let go has lowered service quality, or perhaps there is a board member who insists on implementing or continuing archaic ideas.

Whatever the cause, move on. Life's too short to waste your energy worrying about the past.

Suffocating a good idea

I have had a topic in mind for some time, but kept putting it off because I couldn't settle on a way to frame it. Then one Sunday night I was watching a 60 Minutes story on David Kelley, the founder of a company called IDEO in northern California.

IDEO is a project design firm, but rather than go into all of the products they have designed or improved, you can watch this link to the program. Suffice to say that Steve Jobs was his biggest client and a close friend.

On 60 Minutes, David Kelley talked about how to design breakthrough inventions. He said the key is tossing out ideas and letting others build on them, and then letting others build on that idea, and on and on.

One of the dumbest things I ever did was to keep a good idea under wraps. Because I was so protective of this "baby" of mine, I essentially suffocated it before it had a chance to grow. I was absolutely sure that no one else could be trusted to make the idea work.

I'm telling you this story so that those of you who are reading this do not make the same mistake.

Ladies and Gentlemen, I present to you CyberCIL.com.

When I returned to Arizona in 1995, I began attending Statewide Independent Living Council (SILC) meetings. I had just moved from Pennsylvania, where there are a lot of communities with populations of around 5,000 residents. These communities are clustered together so that a centrally-located CIL could easily serve dozens of these small communities.

In Arizona, however, we have many small communities but they are often separated by at least 50 miles. Placing a center in the middle of these communities wouldn't help anyone.

One day when I was driving home from a SILC meeting, I had a brainstorm. Why not create a virtual CIL? We would not just be a source of I&R, like other centers at that time, we would be an entire organization in cyberspace. No brick and mortar. Our address would be…well…cybercil.org.

About this same time I was approached by Dimenet founder Roland Sykes and another leader in the IL movement about affiliating with each of their organizations. I turned them down, afraid that my idea would be diluted. Roland told me in no uncertain terms that I was being short-sighted. As I look back, he was right.

I launched CyberCIL. I formed a non-profit corporation, recruited a board of directors, found a dedicated volunteer staff member, and made a series of presentations at conferences. Every barrier that we encountered, we overcame. Through CyberCIL, we could offer every service one might receive at a brick and mortar center.

About 10 years ago, enthusiasm for the project began to wane. Funding that I had arranged through the SILC was cut, then disappeared altogether. In spite of the dedication of the volunteer staff member, it was just a matter of time before CyberCIL was gone. It seemed like once I began reducing my involvement, the downward spiral began.

Several IL advocates made valuable, innovative suggestions over the years.

I was so possessive that I didn't share my ideas with others—and allow them to share theirs with me.

Imagine a SILC Congress where a panel of directors of these virtual centers discusses what works and does not work. Imagine how much more effective a CIL's website might be.

If you have a great idea, share it! Let me be the first to thank you.

Dead weight

Almost every center has one. The person who has been on staff since the center opened its doors. The individual's primary value to the agency is to remind everyone about the way things were—and still should be. He or she is strong on the philosophy, but hides behind it to avoid change.

This is your center's expert on leaders who didn't succeed and programs that didn't work. This is the staff person who is quick to tell you about "problem" consumers and problematic regulations, and who dwells on what's wrong but rarely suggests solutions. Performance among people like this is barely adequate, but supervisors let it slide. There may have been warnings or counseling, but no corrective action has ever been taken.

These may have been adequate employees when they were first hired, but as the center changed to meet the changing needs of consumers, these individual did not. The center continues to evolve, but certain employees cling to the past.

When centers continue to employ people like this, they are sending messages to consumers, other staff members, and the community. The CIL is showing consumers that they place a higher priority on protecting employees than giving consumers high quality services. Don't kid yourself--consumers know when staff members aren't doing their jobs and so do other staff members.

Centers that keep paying poor performers are reinforcing substandard work. My sense, even though they would never say it, is that fellow employees actually appreciate it when the organization deals with or dismisses poor performers.

When I consulted with CIL boards and directors, I'd warn them about becoming like sheltered workshops, where employees were paid even though they didn't do their jobs.

Deal with these employees. Don't allow the problem to continue to erode the program. Redirect the person to other opportunities where his or her abilities are a better fit, or let the person go. Just do it.

Is your center a sheltered workshop?

One of the scenarios I like to use in training is about a guy who works in a center and prefers living in an institution because "it's easy." The dilemma for students is whether this Center employee, who is supposed to be a role model for consumers, should be an employee of the center.

In the course of the debate, I often ask whether students felt keeping someone on staff regardless of his or her willingness to do the job made the center no more than a sheltered workshop. After all, we would be paying wages to a person who is not doing the job.

I am always surprised by the number of people would keep this fellow.

This reaction raises a larger issue. Do you have staff members at your center that cannot do their jobs? Are you making excuses for them that perpetuate the idea that people with disabilities cannot do meaningful work? The worst thing we can do to our community is keep employees on who have poor work habits. It sends a message that when you hire a person with a disability, you are taking on a liability. Perhaps this is why our unemployment figures are so high.

Hold employees to their commitments. Set work standards that will be respected in your community and get rid of employees who cannot do their jobs.

Giving negative feedback

We all hate being the bearer of bad news. It's human nature to avoid uncomfortable conversations. But sometimes we need to "bite the bullet" and have a discussion regardless of our fear or discomfort. While negative feedback is never easy to hear, people generally respect those who give it honestly and constructively.

Often, the feedback may be as simple as letting someone know they didn't get a job. If applicants go through an interview process with your organization, you owe them the courtesy of letting them know, personally, about your decision.

Also, a staff member should never be surprised with negative feedback during a performance evaluation. If the employee is not performing well, you need to provide regular coaching to the individual, clearly communicate areas of deficiency, and clear direction about how the employee can improve.

Likewise, we need to be honest with consumers. Sometimes it's as simple as sharing a change in agency procedures that may not be welcomed. Other times it may be feedback on a particular behavior that is driving everyone up the wall.

It's easy in this day of emails and Twitter to feel removed from others. One of the greatest gifts we can give those we do encounter is honest, constructive feedback.

Peer pressure

What do you do if another center in your state doesn't pitch in, or worse, violates an IL principle? If you are like most centers, you do nothing. You might complain to trusted staff or grumble to other center directors. But you never say anything to the violating center director who is ruining the good name of IL.

Rarely is the violation as obvious as a center running a sheltered workshop. More likely, it's a center providing transportation to a sheltered workshop or accepting funds from a business that discriminates against people with disabilities. What should be done about a center that adopts policies or rules that are inconsistent with the law or IL philosophy (such as, "we're not allowed to advocate.")?

Many times, the center's lack of participation is less obvious. They use lobbying restrictions as an excuse for doing nothing. There are centers that never send anyone to the Capitol. They're "too busy." Their consumers complain to your staff and try to get services from other centers.

Rather than looking to the state agency or RSA, take action yourself. State and federal agencies have slow-moving, bureaucratic processes that punish everybody. Do yourself and the other centers a favor and directly approach the culprit. The center director may not like it, but at least you can live with yourself.

Instead of accepting bad conduct that tarnishes the image of all centers, tell the director how you feel. If *we* can't tell our peers the truth, who can?

Tokens

Several years ago I did a lot of training with June Isaacson Kailes, a Disability Policy Consultant. On one occasion, as part of advocacy training, June and I created a piece on "tokenism." Tokenism is not the problem it was 20 years ago, but it still occurs.

It used to occur when people with disabilities allowed themselves to be placed on powerless committees or commissions. This does more harm to the movement than if they did nothing at all. In this day and age, people with disabilities do not have to serve on token committees. We should demand real decision-making authority.

Here are some examples of how a person with a disability can become a token:

1. **Never speaks up, disagrees, or questions** - This person either assumes that he has nothing to offer or is so afraid to rock the boat that he or she holds back.

2. **Allows people to act as if they understand** - This person has something to offer, but others on the committee have difficulty understanding him or her. This may be because of a disability or because the concept is not easily understood by nondisabled people. A token allows people to shake their heads as if they understand when they don't.

3. **Intimidated by credentials or degrees** - This person assumes that others with or without a disability are more knowledgeable because they have more experience or education. This type of intimidation goes back to the days of the medical model.

4. **Allows patronizing attitudes** - Any person with a disability understands this. While most incidents are obvious, some may be more subtle. The only way this is going to stop is when people with disabilities tell others that it is offensive--and why. A token does nothing.

5. **Doesn't try to influence the decision-making process** - Change does not come easy. If you have been appointed to a committee or commission, you have an obligation to represent the needs and interests of people with disabilities in the community and stick up for their rights. Do not be satisfied with merely putting an idea forward. Keep pressing until it is implemented.

6. **Doesn't recruit allies and develop strategies** – If you don't see yourself as an advocate, you won't raise pertinent issues to other advocates. If you don't see your membership on a committee as meaningful, you won't influence others with your knowledge and experience.

7. **Accepts advisory rather than policy-making status** - The key word here is "advisory." If your community has committees that are advisory, they are essentially telling you that someone else has real authority and you are only expected to make recommendations.

8. **Works with the groups that "manage" rather than "assist"** - In Independent Living we assure that consumers are assisted rather than directed. Some organizations created by parents and professionals were designed to meet their own needs rather than the needs of people with disabilities.

9. **Worries more about his or her resume than responsibility to others** - These people allow themselves to be placed on useless committees to impress future employers or organizations with their resumes rather than their accomplishments.

Understanding disability

Experience with disability? "My sister's husband has MS"

When I first worked in the Independent Living Movement, I did not have a disability--or at least not one that was evident. By all accounts, I was one of the good guys. I think that most people with disabilities would have said that I "get it."

Why? Well, I never took the lead when the media came by. I always made sure that my staff members with disabilities were the spokespersons when we were out in the community. I worked to create leaders with disabilities to take over for me when I was away. Although I served on several IL boards, I never ran for an office.

If someone had asked me if I knew what it was like to have a disability, I wouldn't have been so naive as to say "yes." Having had lots of friends with disabilities, however, I probably would have said that I know 80% of what it was like. Friends had talked to me about bowel and bladder care, sexual dysfunction and urinary infections, so I felt like I had a relatively thorough understanding.

Well, I'm here to tell you that I didn't know 20%. I knew a lot of the mechanics and the facts you read in books and articles. But I didn't appreciate how much I didn't know.

I didn't know how it would feel when my former neurologist asked me if I was still working; or when a guy in an elevator looks over at you sadly; or the time someone apologized to me when I carelessly ran over his foot. I didn't know what it felt like the first time you ask someone for an accommodation.

One thing I know now--those little things mean a lot.

Working from home

Not everyone can work from home. Some miss the socialization. Some lack the discipline. Some are too disorganized. Some cannot adapt to today's technology.

The problem with employees who have these needs or deficiencies is that the person who has them often cannot admit to or see them. That places greater responsibility on the supervisor to decide whether to continue. Here are some ways to make it work:

- When setting up the "working-at-home" program, specify that not all jobs can be performed from home (i.e., receptionist, janitor).
- When setting up the program, specify that working at home is not an employee right, and only occurs when both the employee and organization benefit.
- Reverse work at home situations when employee does not meet requirements.
- Make sure that the employee's evaluation includes measurable outcomes. For instance:
    - All consumer files have up-to-date CSRs.
    - All consumer files have either a signed ILP or signed waiver.
    - Records indicate monthly meeting with each peer counseling referral.
    - Employee follows up on each referral within 24 hours.
    - Employee attends 90% of staff meetings either by teleconference or in person.

Bob's Tool Box

POSITION DESCRIPTION

Consumer Directed Care Coordinator

POSITION TITLE: Consumer Directed Care Coordinator
REPORTS TO: Consumer Directed Care Program Manager, Executive Director
POSITION SUMMARY: Works directly with people with disabilities to support their efforts to adapt or maintain an independent lifestyle. Complete assigned responsibilities for the Consumer Directed Care Program with emphasis on assessing consumer needs, developing goals, and providing independent living skills instruction. Incorporates Independent Living Philosophy on a personal and professional level.
MINIMUM REQUIREMENTS: Bachelor's Degree in social sciences or related fields, or combination of 3 years of education and relevant experience.
MAJOR EXPECTATIONS:

- Respond to initial contacts by consumers, contract service providers, family members, social service agencies, and community at large within 5 days.
- Assess and document consumer needs and goals, with emphasis on independent living skills training.
- Understand, apply and administer the LTC/HCBS Waiver, Consumer Directed option in a timely and effective manner.
- Maintain current consumer information, utilizing computer databases and case files.
- Document consumer progress and program activity in a timely manner, keep files and documents current, and complete monthly activity reports as required.
- Makes referrals to other programs or services in the community as appropriate.
- Perform other duties as assigned.

COMPETENCIES:

- Adaptability/Flexibility
  - Respond to changes in methodology and accountability
- Creativity/Innovation:
  - Develop new methods of service provision
- Technical/Functional:
  - High degree of skill in written and oral communication
  - Understand casework principles
  - Considerable knowledge of the causes and effects of various disabilities
  - Computer skills in word processing and databases and knowledge of Office 2000 preferred
- Planning:
  - Set priorities and develop course of action to achieve goals/objectives
- Philosophy:
  - Demonstrate through actions and language an understanding of independent living philosophy

- Travel:
  - Ability to travel to meet with consumers in their home or alternate meeting place within the Care Coordinator's designated sector.
  - Ability to stay overnight out of town when meeting with consumers that do not live near the Coordinator's staff office.
  - Ability to travel to out of town trainings and seminars as necessary
- Other:
  - Complete (number or number of hours), individual program trainings and continuing education classes as directed.
  - Represent (name of CIL) and its programs, staff and directors in a positive, professional manner within the community
  - Maintain a high level of ethics, confidentiality and follow HIPAA laws.
  - Be knowledgeable of and comply with Program policies and procedure
  - Maintain and current and accurate knowledge of relevant programs, benefits and community resources, with an emphasis on Medicaid guidelines and regulations.

Sample Job Description

Major Functions:

Board Administration and Support -- Supports operations and administration of Board by advising and informing Board members, interfacing between Board and staff, and supporting Board's evaluation of chief executive
- Administers the affairs of the corporation directly and indirectly through the supervision of appropriate administrative and/or management staff
- Program, Product and Service Delivery -- Oversees design, marketing, promotion, delivery and quality of programs, products and services
- Financial, Tax, Risk and Facilities Management -- Recommends yearly budget for Board approval and prudently manages organization's resources within those budget guidelines according to current laws and regulations

Human Resource Management -- Effectively manages the human resources of the organization according to authorized personnel policies and procedures that fully conform to current laws and regulations

Community and Public Relations -- Assures the organization and its mission, programs, products, and services are consistently presented in strong, positive image to relevant stakeholders

Fundraising (nonprofit-specific) -- Oversees fundraising planning and implementation, including identifying resource requirements, researching funding sources, establishing strategies to approach funders, submitting proposals and administrating fundraising records and documentation

POSITION DESCRIPTION

Independent Living Advocate

POSITION TITLE: Independent Living Advocate I
REPORTS TO: Unit Manager
POSITION SUMMARY: Works directly with people with disabilities to support their efforts to adapt or maintain an independent lifestyle. Complete assigned responsibilities in the (Name of Unit) with emphasis on assessing consumer needs, developing goals, and providing independent living skills instruction. Incorporates Independent Living Philosophy on a personal and professional level.
MINIMUM REQUIREMENTS: Bachelor's Degree in social sciences or related fields, or combination of 3 years of education and experience. Experience must be in the provision of direct services, preferably to people with disabilities.
MAJOR EXPECTATIONS:
- Respond to initial contacts by consumers, contract service providers, family members, social service agencies, and community at large.
- Assess and document consumer needs and goals, with emphasis on independent living skills training.
- Provide skills training, peer counseling/support, social and recreational assistance, and outreach.
- Maintain current consumer information using computer database.
- Document consumer progress and program activity and submit billing information and required reports.
- Make referrals to other consumer assistance programs or services in the community, as appropriate.
- Perform other duties as assigned.

COMPETENCIES:
- Adaptability/Flexibility:
  - Respond to changes in methodology and accountability.
- Creativity/Innovation:
  - Develop new methods of service provision.
- Technical/Functional:
  - High degree of skill in written and oral communication.
  - Understanding of casework principles.
  - Considerable knowledge of the causes and effects of various disabilities.
  - Computer skills in word processing and databases; knowledge of Office 2000 preferred.
- Planning:
  - Set priorities and develop course of action to achieve goals/objectives.
- Philosophy:
  - Demonstrate through actions and language an understanding of independent living philosophy.

SALARY: (Enter salary or salary range)

Date Revised: (enter date)

Independent Living Specialist

POSITION DESCRIPTION

POSITION TITLE: Independent Living Specialist
REPORTS TO: Independent Living Program Manager, Executive Director
POSITION SUMMARY: Works directly with people with disabilities to support their efforts to adapt or maintain an independent lifestyle. Complete assigned responsibilities for the Independent Living Program with emphasis on assessing consumer needs, developing goals, and providing independent living skills instruction. Incorporates Independent Living Philosophy on a personal and professional level.
MINIMUM REQUIREMENTS: Bachelor's Degree in social sciences or related fields, or combination of 3 years of education and relevant experience.
MAJOR EXPECTATIONS:

- Respond to initial contacts by consumers, contract service providers, family members, social service agencies, and community at large, within 5 days.
- Assess and document consumer needs and goals, with emphasis on independent living skills training.
- Provide skills training, peer counseling/support, social and recreational assistance, and outreach.
- Maintain current consumer information, utilizing computer databases and case files.
- Document consumer progress and program activity in a timely manner, keeps files and documents current, submits funding applications in a timely manner and completes monthly activity reports as required.
- Make referrals to other programs or services in the community as appropriate.
- Perform other duties as assigned.

COMPETENCIES:
Adaptability/Flexibility:

- Respond to changes in methodology and accountability.

Creativity/Innovation:

- Develop new methods of service provision.

Technical/Functional:

- High degree of skill in written and oral communication.
- Understand casework principles.
- Considerable knowledge of the causes and effects of various disabilities.
- Computer skills in word processing and databases; knowledge of Office 2000 preferred.

Planning:

- Set priorities and develop course of action to achieve goals/objectives.

Philosophy:

- Demonstrate through actions and language an understanding of independent living philosophy.

Travel:
- Ability to travel to meet with consumers in their home or alternate meeting place within the Independent Living Specialists' designated sector.
- Ability to stay overnight out of town when meeting with consumers that do not live near the Specialists' staff office.
- Ability to travel to out of town trainings and seminars as necessary

Other:
- Complete (enter number of hours, if applicable) individual program trainings and continuing education classes as directed.
- Represent (Name of organization) and its programs, staff and directors in a positive, professional manner within the community.
- Maintain a high level of ethics, confidentiality and follow HIPAA laws.
- Be Knowledgeable of, and comply with program policies and procedure
- Maintain current and accurate knowledge of relevant programs, benefits and community resources.

Program Manager

POSITION DESCRIPTION

JOB DESCRIPTION
POSITION TITLE: (Enter Program Name) Program Manager
REPORTS TO: Vice President/Director or other Manager
POSITION SUMMARY: Oversee contract compliance, monitor Supervisors' performance and Consumer services. Screen, ad hire employees. Mnitor State and Federal employer guidelines. Conduct (number or type required) trainings.
MINIMUM REQUIREMENTS: Bachelor Degree and/or three years experience in Health Care field. Leadership and/or Management experience. Good communication and organizational skills and computer knowledge.
MAJOR RESPONSIBILITIES:
- Monitor contract compliance: Consumer files, Employee files.
- Monitor ongoing contract compliance: TB test, CPR, 1st Aid, Criminal Clearance Cards and Work Permits.
- Monitor new employee training requirements and ensure all requirements are met prior to employment.
- Recruitment, screen and hire (type of employees).
- Ensure new employees meet all Federal, State and (name of CIL) hiring requirements and guidelines.
- Oversee compliance of Federal, State and Local labor laws.
- Review employee Criminal Background check and take appropriate action.
- Monitor Supervisor contract compliance; New Consumer on-site intake/assessment and Consumer Service Agreement, Consumer Service Evaluations; 5, 30 60, 90 days and every 90 days thereafter.
- Monitor new 5 day Competency Evaluations/Consumer Satisfaction Evaluation. Complete annual Performance Evaluations and Supervisor consumer/employee notes/documentation.
- Monitor Supervisor to provide appropriate referrals to consumers.
- Assist Supervisor to resolve employee/consumer conflicts when necessary; ensure issues are reviewed, investigated and plan of action is in place that will prevent reoccurrence. Review Supervisor's Incident Report.
- Monitor consumer and employee data entry is completed according to policies and procedures.
- Monitor Supervisor and employees to ensure PAS and other policies and procedures are being enforced.
- Evaluate program to determine effectiveness and need for modification.
- Establish and maintain cooperative and effective working relationships with ALTCS Case Managers and other agencies.
- Participate and takes initiative in development of program goals, objectives and strategies.
- Set project priorities and develop course of action to achieve goals/objectives/ strategies.

Competencies:
Adaptability/flexibility:
- Assumes a wide range of assignments and responsibilities.

Creativity/Innovation:
- Identifies improved methods for record keeping, file maintenance, computerization of new records and forms

Technical/Functional:
- Knowledge of office machines and computer operations.
- Appropriate use of grammar and spelling.

Interpersonal:
- Works cooperatively and effectively with other to achieve XXXX's goals.

Philosophical:
- Demonstrates an understanding of independent living philosophy through action and language.

Salary: $50,000 to 60,000

VAN DRIVER

JOB DESCRIPTION

JOB TITLE: Van Driver
REPORTS TO: (Enter position name)
RESPONSIBILITIES:
- Primary Van Driver for (Name of CIL/Program(s)
- Provide direct transportation services to consumers in the agency vehicle;
- Assist agency staff in the performance of tasks related to the provision of transportation services to consumers.
- Collect and evaluate information pertaining to the use of the vehicle.
- Ensure that the vehicle is locked and parked in appropriate parking space.
- Exercise good judgment and perform within the local, state and federal guidelines established for the operation of a vehicle.
- Assist in organizing and charting routes that will be cost effective and time efficient.
- Responsible for oil, water, tires and windshield maintenance as well as the overall cleanliness of the van. Routine maintenance can be performed by a paid vendor
- Establish courier routine to deliver mail, checks, gloves, etc. to satellite offices.

KNOWLEDGE, ABILITIES AND SKILLS:
- Must have some knowledge and experience transporting persons with disabilities in a similar type vehicle, including operating a wheelchair lift and securement system.
- Knowledge of the metropolitan area and ability to read and follow maps.
- Good knowledge of agency's policies and procedures related to the operation of the vehicle, and general knowledge in the areas of vehicle maintenance and operation in the State of (name of state).
- Skill in interpersonal relationships as applied to interaction with consumers, staff, tenants and the general public. Must be able to communicate effectively.
- Computer skills.

MINIMUM REQUIREMENTS:
Driver must possess and keep current a (name of state) driver's license and have a clean driving record. CDL license preferred. Driver will provide (name of organization) with a current Motor Vehicle Record and continue to provide annual updates of such record. Basic hours 8:00 a.m.-5:00 p.m. but must be able to work flexible schedule.

Revised (Date)

Executive Director Planning Tool and Evaluation

Executive Director Name: _____

Please rate the job performance of the Executive Director on a scale of 1 to 5 as follows:

5 = Outstanding/distinguished performance (consistently exceeds the basic job responsibilities and expectations.)

4 = Exceed standards/commendable performance (often exceeds the basic job responsibilities and expectations.)

3 = Satisfactory performance (consistently meets the basic job responsibilities and expectations.)

2 = Partially met standards/marginal performance/needs improvement (needs improvement to meet the basic job responsibilities and expectations.)

1 = Performance does not meet job standards/unsatisfactory (fails to meet the basic job responsibilities and expectations. Significant improvement must be demonstrated.)

Expectation	Rating
Philosophy	
I. Program philosophy	
5 = Organization's grants and contracts assure that IL Philosophy is integrated into the operations of every program	
3= One or more of organization's grants and contracts do not address IL Philosophy.	
1= One or more of organization's grants and contracts violate IL Philosophy.	
II. Staff philosophy	
5= All staff receive IL philosophy training annually. Records and staff interviews indicate that staff practices IL philosophy.	
3= Records and staff interviews indicate that staff practice IL philosophy.	
1= Records and staff interviews reveal 3 or more instances where staff do not integrate IL philosophy into their practice.	
III. Organization operations	

5= Organization facilities, programs, and services are always 100% accessible.	
3= Organization receives 2 or fewer justified (as determined by the board chair) accessibility complaints annually.	
1= Organization receives 4 or more justified (as determined by the board chair) accessibility complaints annually.	
IV. Advocacy	
5= Most board members agree that the Executive Director is conversant on all aspects of local, state, and national issues and legislation impacting people with disabilities.	
3= Most board members agree that the Executive Director is conversant on issues or legislation, but not both.	
1= Most board members agree that the Executive Director is not conversant on local, state, and national issues and legislation impacting people with disabilities.	
V. Leadership	
5= Executive Director and organization are recognized by local, state, and national policymakers as primary authority on issues impacting disability community.	
3= Organization is recognized by local, state, and national policymakers as primary authority on issues impacting disability community.	
1= Consumers report that they do not perceive organization as a primary authority on issues impacting disability community.	
VI. Collaboration	
5= Developed and coordinated efforts to work with other disability rights organizations at a state and/or national basis to promote the rights of people with disabilities and their families.	
3= Developed coalitions with other organizations and groups around issues to address training needs, legislative agendas and supports to communities.	
1= Did not attempt to create coalitions or participate in them.	
Administration	
I. Organization has an independent audit	

5= Organization completed annual audit with no major exceptions and presentation was made to board.	
3= Audit revealed at least one major exception and/or presentation was not made to board.	
1= Annual audit was not completed.	
II. Financial reports	
5= Current balance sheet and updated schedule of revenues and expenses were presented at each board meeting.	
3= Current balance sheet and updated schedule of revenues and expenses were not presented at one board meeting.	
1= Current balance sheet and updated schedule of revenues and expenses were not presented at more than one board meeting.	
III. Grant/contract reports	
5= All grant and contract reports were submitted within the required timelines.	
3= One or more grant and/or contract reports were not submitted within the required timelines.	
1= One or more grant and/or contract reports were not submitted within the required timelines resulting in a loss of revenue to the organization.	
IV. Organizational austerity	
5= All policies, procedures, reports, documentation, and activities were reviewed, monitored, and updated to assure the integrity of the organization.	
3= One or more policies or procedures was not reviewed and/or updated annually.	
1= One or more incidents occurred during the evaluation period which jeopardized the operations of the organization.	
V. Resource development	
5= Wrote grants and negotiates contracts which increase organization budget by 10% during fiscal year.	
3= Wrote grants and negotiates contracts which maintain organization budget during fiscal year.	

1= Organization budget decreased by more than 10% during fiscal year.	
VI. Short and long range planning	
5= Assisted board in tracking short and long range goals and objectives.	
3= Assured that staff carried out strategies identified in short and long range plans.	
1= Failure to assure that staff carried out strategies identified in short and long range plans resulted in goal that was neither met nor revised.	
VII. Board communication	
5= All board members believe Executive Director facilitates discussion, keeps board informed, and makes sound recommendations.	
3= Majority of board members believe Executive Director facilitates discussion, keeps board informed, and makes sound recommendations.	
1= More than 2 board members believe Executive Director does not facilitate discussion, does not keep board informed, and does not makes sound recommendations.	
VIII. Board direction	
5= All board believe Executive Director accepts constructive criticism, is receptive to board member ideas and suggestions, and follows up on all problems and issues brought to his attention.	
3= Majority of board believe Executive Director accepts constructive criticism, is receptive to board member ideas and suggestions, and follows up on all problems and issues brought to his attention.	
1= More than 2 of board members believe Executive Director does not accept constructive criticism, is not receptive to board member ideas and suggestions, and does not follow up on all problems and issues brought to his attention.	
Supervision	
I. Evaluations	
5= All staff in organization were formally evaluated during the evaluation year.	
3= All directly supervised staff were formally evaluated during the evaluation year.	

1= Two or more directly supervised staff were not formally evaluated during the evaluation year.	
II. Personnel development	
5= Each staff member has a personalized plan for professional growth.	
3= Recruits, trains, and supervises personnel to fulfill grant and contract requirements.	
1= Staff turnover results in inability for fulfill requirements of grants and contracts.	
III. Morale	
5= All staff randomly selected and interviewed report that they view employment in this organization as a valuable step in their professional development.	
3= All staff randomly selected and interviewed report that they are treated fairly, well-informed about organizational changes, policies and procedures, and employed in an effective work environment	
1= Board receives two or more justified grievances against Executive Director	
IV. Decision-making	
5= All staff randomly selected and interviewed report that they are rewarded for thoughtful acts of initiative and creativity.	
3= All staff randomly selected and interviewed report that they are encouraged to be creative and innovative when performing their jobs and supported regardless of the outcome.	
1= Staff randomly selected and interviewed report that they are punished for deviating from traditional practices and procedures.	
V. Employment law	
5= Organization tried at least two innovative approaches that protect employees while expanding assistance to persons with disabilities.	
3= Ability to address all employment issues confronting organization indicated knowledge and awareness of employment law.	
1= Organization consistently lost decisions about worker's comp and unemployment	

VI. Delegation	
5= All directly-supervised staff believe Executive Director gives clear directions and delegates authority appropriate to program needs and the capacity of individuals.	
3= Majority of directly-supervised staff believe Executive Director gives clear directions and delegates authority appropriate to program needs and the capacity of individuals.	
1= Majority of directly-supervised staff believe Executive Director does not give clear directions and does not delegate authority appropriate to program needs and the capacity of individuals.	

Board Comments: (Please comment on duties the employee has performed outside those identified in this evaluation (attach additional sheets if necessary).

_____
_____
_____
_____
_____
_____
_____

Executive Director Remarks:

_____
_____
_____
_____
_____
_____
_____

Planner: This document will be used to evaluate the performance of the Executive Director during the period _____ to _____.

_____
Signature: Board of Directors Chairperson   Date

_____
Signature: Executive Director   Date

Evaluation:

_____
Signature: Board of Directors Chairperson   Date

Signature: Executive Director   Date
(Employee signature does not necessarily indicate that the employee agrees with this evaluation. Employee may attach comments.)

The Executive Director Planning Tool and Evaluation was created by Bob Michaels as a resource for centers for independent living. It may be reproduced without permission,

FREQUENTLY ASKED QUESTIONS ABOUT LOBBYING AND CILS

Revised 1998
by Bob Michaels

"It's easy to tell if a center's doing strong advocacy. Someone from the state is telling them they're not allowed to lobby."
--Ed Roberts

This FAQ addresses lobbying questions raised during our training programs, technical assistance calls, and consultant work. It was originally developed in May 1997 and revised in response to amendments made to OMB Circular A-122 in 1998.

In developing this FAQ, a study was conducted of pertinent regulations of the Internal Revenue Service and the Department of Education, and then the answers were reviewed with an attorney specializing in lobbying issues and with John Nelson, chief of Independent Living Branch of Rehabilitation Services Administration and other officials of the Department of Education. We hope you find this FAQ useful, and we welcome any recommendations for improving it.

1. Are centers for independent living allowed to lobby?

Yes, CILs may lobby; however, the types of lobbying activities that are permissible vary, depending on whether they are supported with federal or non-federal funds. In addition, a CIL's lobbying activities may be further limited by Internal Revenue Service regulations applicable to nonprofit organizations.

2. What statutes or regulations do centers need to follow with regard to lobbying?

- The federal government requires granting and contracting agencies, such as the Department of Education, to follow guidelines set out in the Office of Management and Budget (OMB) Circular A-122 (as amended in August 1997) when awarding federal funds. Additional restrictions may be found in Department of Education regulations 34 CFR Part 82.
- Centers may elect to follow guidelines set out in regulations developed under the Internal Revenue Code, Sections 501(h) and 4911.
- Centers which employ lobbyists or direct considerable funds to lobbying activities must meet reporting requirements set out in the Lobbying Disclosure Act of 1995 (P.L. 104-65).

While requirements contained in these three documents will be covered in the remainder of this FAQ, there may be other federal, state, or local laws or regulations which affect the lobbying activities of a center. Center staff should contact agencies in their states which regulate activities of nonprofits and request provisions related to lobbying activities.

It is imperative that center staff have a thorough understanding of these laws and regulations whenever issues of compliance are raised—and always get a second opinion.

3. I have been told that centers receiving Title VII funds are restricted from lobbying. Is this true?

Except as described in #5 below, CILs that receive Title VII funds are restricted from using Title VII as well as other federal funds to engage in lobbying activities. However, as stated above, centers may use nonfederal funds to engage in lobbying activities.

4. What lobbying activities may not be supported with federal funds?

Briefly, lobbying activities that cannot be supported with federal funds include:

- Attempts to influence the outcome of any federal, state, or local election, referendum, initiative, or similar procedure.
- Supporting in any way a political party, campaign, political action committee, or other organization established for the purpose of influencing the outcome of elections.
- Any attempt to influence the introduction, enactment, or modification of federal or state legislation, including efforts to utilize state or local officials to engage in similar activities.
- Any attempt to influence the introduction, enactment, or modification of federal or state legislation by trying to gain the support of part or all of the general public.
- Legislative liaison activities in support of unallowable lobbying activities.
- Any attempt to influence an executive or legislative branch official with respect to any grant, contract, loan, or cooperative agreement.

It is important to note that activities that may not be supported by a center's federal funds may be supported by its nonfederal funds.

5. What lobbying activities may be supported with federal funds?

Non-restricted lobbying activities (that is, those lobbying activities which can be supported with federal funds) include:

- Providing a presentation through hearing testimony, statements, or letters in response to a documented request, if the information needed for the presentation is readily available. Costs for travel, lodging, and meals are not allowed unless testimony is given in response a written request from the chairman or ranking minority member of a Congressional committee or subcommittee.
- Lobbying to influence state legislation, in order to reduce directly the cost of performing the grant or contract or to avoid impairing the organization's ability to do so.

- Any activity specifically authorized by statute to be undertaken with funds from the grant, contract, or other agreement.

6. Will we jeopardize our center's 501(c)(3) status if we lobby?

There are really two questions that must be answered: (1) Is the activity under consideration really lobbying; and (2) does lobbying constitute a substantial portion of what the center does under IRS rules.

Question One: Are the center's activities lobbying or something else?

Direct lobbying is defined in the Internal Revenue Code (IRC) and regulations as "Any attempt to influence any legislation through communication with any member or employee of a legislative body or with any government official or employee who may participate in the formulation of the legislation."

This includes such obvious activities as contact with a legislator about a specific piece of legislation, advocating for increases in funding in the budget, opposing a candidate for appointive office, and encouraging the general public to support or reject an initiative, referendum, or board measure.

Direct lobbying does not include activities such as educating decision makers about issues of importance to people with disabilities, administrative lobbying, surveying candidates for office, attending public hearings, or even testifying if requested by a legislative committee in writing. Nonpartisan analysis and self-defense lobbying also qualify as exceptions under IRS rules.

A communication (with the general public or any segment thereof) will be treated as grass roots lobbying if, and only if, the communication (1) refers to specific legislation, (2) reflects a view on such legislation, and (3) encourages the recipient to take action with respect to such legislation (for instance, through a "call to action").

Question Two: Is lobbying a substantial part of what the center does?

Centers can either elect to comply with IRC Section 501(h), which requires filing papers with the IRS and reporting annually on lobbying activities, or elect not to file under the law. Compliance with the law allows 501(c)(3) corporations to expend as much as 20 percent of their funds for lobbying activities depending on the size of the organization. Those choosing not to file can only spend an amount that is not "substantial." One court ruled that devoting more than five percent of an organization's resources to lobbying activities was substantial.

So, why doesn't everyone file under IRC 501(h)? Because most organizations haven't learned about it yet. The guidelines are far more generous, yet record-keeping demands for day-to-day lobbying activities are virtually the same.

7. How does lobbying differ from advocacy?

In the regulations for Title VII of the Rehab Act, advocacy is defined as "pleading an individual's cause or speaking or writing in support of an individual. . . . Advocacy may be on behalf of a single individual . . . a group or class of individuals . . . or oneself." Note that in this context, "pleading" is a legal term meaning "a formal statement setting forth the defense of a case" (Random House Dictionary). Advocacy, then, is action taken to convince others of the rightness of your cause and of their need to join you in supporting this cause. Lobbying is a subset of advocacy, in that it is a set of activities that plead a cause and set forth the defense of a case in order to influence the voting of legislators. In other words, lobbying is advocacy with a very narrow and specific focus-- to convince legislators to vote as you wish them to on specific legislative proposals. Thus, the use of the word "advocacy" does not change the nature of what is or is not permitted as a lobbying activity.

8. Where can our center get more information about compliance with the Internal Revenue Code?

You can always try the IRS itself, but most of its information is not written for people other than certified public accountants. One excellent source of information we've found has been written by Greg Colvin, an attorney who specializes in this area. You can contact Greg at Silk, Adler, and Colvin 415.421.7555 to inquire about resource materials he has developed regarding lobbying and the tax code. Other sources include Independent Sector (1828 L, N.W., 1200, Washington, D.C., 20036, 202.223.8100); Alliance for Justice (2000 P St., N.W., Suite 712, Washington, D.C. 20036, 202.822.6070); and Chronicle of Philanthropy (1255 23rd Street, N.W., Suite 700, Washington, D.C., 20037, 202.466.1200).

9. How does the Lobbying Disclosure Act of 1995 affect centers?

In most cases, it doesn't. Centers that attempt to influence Congress or top federal executive branch officials may be required to register, to report their areas of interest, and to specify the amount of money spent on lobbying activities. A center is required to register under the Act only if: 1) an individual employed or retained by the center makes more than one contact and spends 20 percent or more of his or her time providing lobbying activities for the center during a six month period; and 2) the center's total expenses in connection with lobbying activities exceed $20,000 in a six month period.

10. How may I obtain copies of the documents identified in this FAQ?

The documents referred to in this FAQ are available through the Government Printing Office or from your auditor or congressman. In addition, many codes, regulations, and legislation can be downloaded electronically from the Internet.

- To access OMB Circular A-122 online, go directly to www.whitehouse.gov/WH/EOP/OMB/html/circulars/a122/a122.html

- For the Internal Revenue Code (P.L. 94-455), the address is www.law.cornell.edu/uscode/26/4955.html
- To find a copy of the Lobbying Disclosure Act of 1995 (P.L. 104-65) Act and other federal legislation, go to the Thomas homepage at http://thomas.loc.gov, probably the best springboard into everything from public documents to the inner workings of Congress.

CONCLUSION

As you know, advocacy is one of the core services of a center, essential to achieving the mission of promoting independent living opportunities for persons with disabilities. This said, among the questions most often heard by IL NET trainers and technical assistants are what constitutes advocacy and what distinguishes it from lobbying? This FAQ is intended to provide the basics. If you need more information, be sure to contact an attorney or your grantor agency.

This fact sheet was prepared by Bob Michaels with assistance from Laurel Richards, Cynthia Dresden, and Dawn Heinsohn. We extend our appreciation to Greg Colvin, John Nelson of the Independent Living Branch, RSA, Sergio Kapfer, Department of Education General Attorney, Division of Educational Equity and Research, and Susan Winchell, Department of Education Ethics Counsel Staff for agreeing to review these responses.

Revised March 1998

FREQUENTLY ASKED QUESTIONS
ABOUT MULTIPLE CHEMICAL SENSITIVITY

1998
by Bob Michaels

1. What is Multiple Chemical Sensitivity?

Multiple Chemical Sensitivity (MCS) is a condition in which individuals become ill following exposure to certain chemicals encountered in everyday life. Such chemicals include smoke, pesticides, plastics, synthetic fabrics, perfumes, scented products, petroleum products, fumes, and paints.

Individuals who experience MCS have a more intense reaction to chemicals than most people, in much the same way some individuals have a far more severe allergic reaction to animals or pollen.

2. How is MCS related to Environmental Illness (EI)?

MCS is acute sensitivity to chemical substances. EI includes not only this but also a broad range of conditions triggered by airborne pollution, food, naturally occurring substances such as molds and pollens, and electromagnetic fields.

3. How common is MCS?

According to recent studies, approximately 15 percent of the population has increased sensitivity to chemicals. It is estimated that physicians have diagnosed five percent of people in the United States, or about 13 million people, as being especially vulnerable to certain common chemicals. There have been several recent studies, cited below, which support these findings.

The incidence of MCS seems to be higher with women than men (as is the case with many autoimmune diseases), often appears between the ages of 30 and 50 years, and strikes without regard to race or economic background.

4. What causes MCS?

It is not precisely clear what causes MCS. Sometimes a single incident such as petrochemical fire can trigger MCS. Often, a reaction intensifies without warning but with grave effects. Commonly cited examples of MCS development include recurrent exposure to fresh paint, pest control insecticides, and carpeting glue. Research on MCS has also indicated that long-term exposure to chemicals has a cumulative effect on many people.

There are other factors that may contribute or predispose a person to MCS. These include heredity, nutrition, hormonal functioning, presence of another illness, some medications, trauma, and stress.

5. Is MCS real--or just a psychosomatic, "boutique" disability?

People with disabilities have a long history of needing to convince physicians, researchers, and even family members that they experience very real ailments. Most recently, people with Multiple Sclerosis, Gulf War Syndrome, and Post Polio Syndrome had long intense battles with physicians to convince them that the incapacitation they experience is not "in their heads," or a manifestation of a "poor attitude."

Both MCS and EI are very real conditions, even though many medical doctors are not yet trained to identify this disability. The Social Security Administration and U.S. Department of Housing and Urban Development recognize MCS as a disabling condition, as do numerous other government agencies and judicial bodies.

Some advocates refer to this disability as Chemical Injury Syndrome (CIS), which they believe more effectively communicates the severity of this disability.

6. What architectural design standards must be followed to make my center more accessible to persons with MCS and EI?

The short answer is--there aren't any. Neither the Uniform Federal Accessibility Standards (UFAS) nor the Americans with Disabilities Act Accessibility Guidelines for Buildings and Facilities (ADAAG) address MCS and EI.

Centers for independent living often set a higher standard of accessibility, exceeding the requirements of the law. Center boards, staff, and consumers know all too well the frustration one feels when confronted with the excuses like, "they don't come in here anyway" and "it costs too much." Centers must set an example in assuring that all people can enter their offices.

7. What can we do to make our facility (center) more accessible to persons with MCS and EI?

Here are ten recommendations that will make your facility accessible to most people with MCS/EI:

- Adopt and enforce no smoking and no fragrance policies and post signs accordingly, including on paths of travel (to restrooms, the parking lot, common areas, etc).
- Discontinue chemical pest control, such as structural chemicals and flea bombs, and replace them with non-toxic pest controls. (Sources for alternative products are identified below.)
- Remove or disarm fragrance emission devices and systems (FEDS).

- Discontinue using toxic, fragrance-laden cleaning products, and use only non-toxic paints on the walls and ceilings.
- Attach carpeting to floors using nails or adhesive strips rather than glue; ventilate thoroughly.
- Prohibit staff and visitors from idling vehicles near the entranceway or windows of the facility.
- Purchase only metal and real wood furniture (look for used furniture) and avoid synthetic cloth-covered room dividers and curtains that collect dust and contaminants.
- Landscape with ornamental rock and pebbles. Avoid juniper, olive, acacia, and cedar trees. Discontinue use of lawn care chemicals.
- Incorporate notice of your MCS/EI safeguards into all center literature and correspondence. Here is an example: "To allow The Center for Independent Living to be fully accessible to all people with disabilities, including persons with multiple chemical sensitivities/environmental illness, please do not wear scented products (perfume, aftershave, deodorant, shampoo, etc.) to any meetings, demonstrations, groups, or workshops held at or by the CIL. We appreciate your cooperation. Meetings are wheelchair accessible, and assistive listening devices, as well as materials in alternate formats, are available upon request."
- At minimum, make one room "safe,"--that is, create an environmentally safe room with a separate entranceway, if possible. This well-ventilated room would be free of carpeting, curtains, fluorescent lights, microwave oven, electromagnetic fields, natural gas, and toxins.

8. Where can I get more information about MCS and EI?

This FAQ has borrowed heavily from two documents: Topics, Multiple Chemical Sensitivity, prepared by Beth Pifer of the Arizona Technology Access Program (AZTAP) and Multiple Chemical Sensitivity by Ann McCampbell, M.D.

Other sources for help, information, local resources, and alternative products are listed below.

ADDITIONAL READING/INFORMATION

American Academy of Environmental Medicine
P.O. Box 1001-8001
New Hope, PA 18938
(215) 862-4544
FAX: 862-2418

American Indian Environmental Illness Foundation
Terri Hansen, Director
P.O. Box 1039
Long Beach, WA 98631
(360) 665-3913

Arizona Technology Access Program
Northern Arizona University
Institute for Human Development
P.O. Box 5630
Flagstaff, AZ 86011-5630
(800) 553-0718
(520) 523-4791
TTY: 523-1695
FAX: 523-9127

Iris R. Bell, MD
Tucson VA Medical Center
3601 South Sixth Avenue
Mail Slot 4-116A Tucson, AZ 85723
(520) 792-1450 ext. 5127

Chemical Injury Information Network
Cynthia Wilson, Director
P.O. Box 301
White Sulphur Springs, MT 59645
(406) 547-2255

The Dispossessed Project
Rhonda Zwillinger
P.O. Box 402
Paulden, AZ 86334-0402
(520) 636-2802

Environmental Research Foundation
105 Eastern Avenue, Suite 101
Annapolis, MD 21403-3300
(410) 263-1584

The Guide to Planning Accessible Meetings
c/o ILRU Program
2323 S. Shepherd, Suite 1000
Houston, TX 77019
(713) 520-0232
TTY: 520-5136

The Labor Institute
853 Broadway, Room 2014
New York, NY 10003
(212) 674-3322

MCS Referral and Resources
Albert Donnay, Director
508 Westgate Road
Baltimore, MD 21229-2343
(410) 362-6400
FAX: 362-6401

National Center for Environmental Health Strategies (NCEHS)
Mary Lamielle, Director
1100 Rural Avenue Voorhees, NJ 08043
(609) 429-5358

NY Coalition for Alternatives to Pesticides (NYCAP)
353 Hamilton
Albany, NY 12210
(518) 426-8246
FAX: 426-3052

CONSUMER ORIENTATION

Electrical Sensitivity Network
Lucinda Grant, Director
P.O. Box 4146
Prescott, AZ 86302-4146
(520) 778-4637

The Environmental Health Network
P.O. Box 1155
Larkspur, CA 94977
(415) 541-5075

Human Ecology Action League (HEAL) of Southern Arizona
PO Box 36404
Tucson AZ 85740-6404
(520) 797-4585

National Coalition for the Chemically Injured
Susan Molloy
HC-63 Box 7195
Snowflake, AZ 85937
(520) 536-4625

GOVERNMENT AGENCIES

US Department of Housing and Urban Development (HUD)
Office of Fair Housing and Equal Opportunity
1-800-669-9777
US Social Security Administration
1-800-772-1213

ALTERNATIVE INSECT CONTROL

Pristine Products
Chuck Hadd
2311 East Indian School Road
Phoenix, AZ 85016
(800) 216-4968
(602) 955-7031
FAX: 955-1812

William Currie
P.O. Box 2469
Prescott, AZ 86304-2469
(520) 776-7782

CONCLUSION

This fact sheet was prepared by Bob Michaels with assistance from Laurel Richards, Dawn Heinsohn, and Agnes McAllister. Appreciation is extended to Susan Molloy who contributed significantly to this document.

IL History & Philosophy

1. History of Independent Living, by Gina McDonald and Mike Oxford
   http://www.cilww.com/pdf/History-of-Independent-Living.pdf

2. IL History and Philosophy: Orientation for IL Staff, (4 Videos and Study guide)
   http://www.ilru.org/il-history-and-philosophy-orientation-for-il-staff

3. A Little History Worth Knowing, (22 min. film)
   http://www.ilru.org/il-video-lending-library

4. How IL History and Philosophy Shape Our Future, (teleconference)
   http://ncsilc.org/wp-content/uploads/2013/03/How-IL-History-and-Philosophy-Shape-Our-Future-training-manual.pdf

5. History of Independent Living, (RapidCourses)
   http://www.ilru.org/training/foundations-independent-living-series-4

6. The Great Fight for Disability Rights
   http://www.storylinemotionpictures.com/

7. Lives worth Living
   http://www.storylinemotionpictures.com/LivesWorthLiving.htm

Links

- Board Training for Centers
  http://ilru.mediasite.com/mediasite/Catalog/Full/dc5a30b5c2ab4094b806de3d4a7
  77e3221#dc5a30b5c2ab4094b806de3d4a777e3221/?state=qouiVhIXu8anGtU7
  U0Cx&_suid=109

- CIL Outcome Measures
  https://drive.google.com/?usp=chrome_app#folders/0B2vJ29p4Zi7KaVFIUUpkZ
  HZVWEk

- Introduction to SILCs: 101
  http://ilru.mediasite.com/mediasite/Catalog/Full/d32c18193f4a4811874335a781c
  d836421

- Orientation for New CIL and SILC Personnel – ONP1
  http://ilru.mediasite.com/mediasite/Catalog/Full/a5e6e6fdfadf450f9589f54aae054
  da921

- Scenarios
  https://drive.google.com/?usp=chrome_app#folders/0B2vJ29p4Zi7KcDhSWlRUM
  mZHbTA

- SILC Job Descriptions
  https://drive.google.com/?usp=chrome_app#folders/0B2vJ29p4Zi7KQktpOWgwd
  VpRRzA

- Try Another Way
  http://mn.gov/mnddc/parallels2/four/video/video44-tryanotherway.html

SILC Quiz

__F__1. The VR agency must approve all appointments to the SILC.

__T__2. Fifty-one percent or more of the members of the SILC must be people with disabilities.

__F__3. Every SILC must have a member of the business community on it.

__F__4. The SILC must include members from all of the major disability groups.

__F__5. Only one center for independent living (CIL) director may serve on the council at any one time.

__T__6. The governor appoints the director representing the CILs.

__T__7. The governor may delegate the authority to re-appoint the members of the Council to the SILC.

__T__8. The governor must appoint people who are knowledgeable about CILs.

__F__9. The governor no longer makes the appointments if a SILC becomes a non-profit organization.

__F__10. Employees of the state are never allowed to vote on SILC business.

__F__11. The SILC may identify a temporary member to sit on the Council if the governor fails to make the appointment.

__F__12. CIL directors are not allowed to vote on SILC business.

__F__13. The SILC members always select the chairperson of the SILC.

__F__14. The representative of the designated state agency may serve as the chairperson of the SILC.

__T__15. There must be at least one member of the SILC on the Rehabilitation Council.

__F__16. Members who have completed their terms cannot be re-appointed for one year.

__F__ 17. Center representatives may not chair the SILC.

__T__ 18. The SILC determines where in the state the next new center will be located.

__F__ 19. One of the duties of the SILC is to identify ineffective providers of IL services and remove them from the service system.

__F__ 20. Each on-site compliance review of a center must include a representative of the SILC.

__T__ 21. The SILC may pay a member for performing council duties.

__F__ 22. The SILC may not start assembling the SPIL until 12 months before it is due.

__T__ 23. The SILC and designated state agency develop the State Plan for IL together.

__F__ 24. The State Plan must include at least one objective for the use of Chapter 2 (Older-Blind) funds.

__T__ 25. The SILC must hold public hearings while it is putting the plan together.

__F__ 26. The SILC is responsible for monitoring the centers in its state.

__T__ 27. Part B funds are distributed by the State VR Agency.

__T__ 28. Part C funds are to be used for the operation of CILs.

__T__ 29. Social Security Reimbursement Funds may be used for programs in Title VII.

__T__ 30. Funds allotted by the state for the operation of CILS must be included in the State Plan for IL.

__F__ 31. Social Security Reimbursement Funds which are used for the operation of centers may be considered state contributions when determining whether or not a state is eligible for 723 status.

__T__ 32. State designated agencies may use part of their state's allotment for VR to support the SILC.

__F__ 33. SILCs may never lobby.

__T__ 34. A state loses its federal IL funding if the SILC fails to submit a SPIL.

__F__35. SILC staff may be employees of the state, but they must work exclusively for the Council.

2/13   The *SILC Quiz* was created by Bob Michaels as a learning tool for SILC members. It may be reproduced without permission, but please credit the author.

The Exit Interview

- What caused you to resign?
- Was a single event responsible for your decision to leave?
- What do you value about the SILC?
- What did you dislike about the SILC?
- The quality of supervision is important to most people at work. How was your relationship with your chairs?
- What could I have done to improve my management style and skill?
- What did you like most about your job?
- What did you dislike about your job? What would you change about your job?
- Do you feel you had the resources and support necessary to accomplish your job? If not, what was missing?
- We try to be an employee-oriented organization in which employees experience positive morale and motivation. What is your experience of employee morale and motivation in the company?
- Were your job responsibilities characterized correctly during the interview process and orientation?
- Did you have clear goals and know what was expected of you in your job?
- Did you receive adequate feedback about your performance day-to-day and in the performance development planning process?
- Did you clearly understand and feel a part of the accomplishment of the company mission and goals?
- Did the management of the SILC care about and help you accomplish your personal and professional development and career goals?
- What would you recommend to help us create a better workplace?
- Do the policies and procedures of the SILC help to create a well-managed, consistent, and fair workplace in which expectations are clearly defined?
- Describe the qualities and characteristics of the person who is most likely to succeed in this company.
- What are the key qualities and skills we should seek in your replacement?
- Do you have any recommendations regarding our compensation, benefits and other reward and recognition efforts?
- Would you recommend the company as a good place to work to your friends and family?
- Can you offer any other comments that will enable us to understand why you are leaving, how we can improve, and what we can do to become a better SILC?

EMPLOYEE NAME:

DATE OF INTERVIEW:

1. Were you compensated in accordance to your agreement with SILC?
   Yes_____
   No_____

2. Have you provided service to SILC for which you have not yet received compensation?
   Yes_____
   No_____
   (If yes, please explain in comment section.)

3. Have you experienced any on the job injury for which you may require treatment?
   Yes_____
   No_____
   (If yes, please explain in comment section.)

4. Do you have any physical or intellectual property, equipment or software in your possession that belongs to SILC?
   Yes_____
   No_____

5. Have you turned in all of your keys?
   Yes_____
   No_____

6. Do you have any SILC files/property in your possession?
   Yes_____
   No_____

COMMENTS:_____

_____

_____

Please Sign and Date.

_____   _____
Employee Signature   Date

_____
Interviewer's Signature, Title

The Fog Index

1. Count off 100 words in the written material you want to test. Do not use more than 100 words because the formula will not work if you do. (Well, give or take a word-- but stop with the sentence that ends <u>closest to 100</u>).

2. Figure out the average length of the sentences in your 100 word sample. To do this, simply count the number of sentences, and divide your total number of words by the sentence total. For instance, if two sentences are made up of 104 words, then the average sentence length is 52 words.

3. Next, count the number of hard words, which Gunning defines as any word with three or more syllables. Do not count capitalized words (like the Department of Education, Pennsylvania, etc.), words that are combinations of short, easy words like bookkeeper or housewife, or words that have a suffix such as expect<u>ed</u>, deserv<u>ing</u>, or heaven<u>ly</u>.

4. Finally, add the number of "hard" words to the average sentence length obtained earlier. Then multiply the sum by 0.4. This will give you the FOG INDEX. The sum relates directly to school grade reading level. So if your final score is 16.2, this would mean that your memo would be best understood by someone who has completed at least 16 grades (a college senior or graduate of college).

In an intensive study of several large organizations, Mr. Gunning found that most written directives score in the 20s and 30s which essentially means <u>anyone</u> would have problems reading the document and coming away with a clear understanding. I honestly cannot explain how this formula works--you'll have to read the book!!!

THE LOBBYING TEST

Identify whether or not the following activities would be in violation of lobbying laws or regulations.

LOBBYING

1. Communication with a legislator or public official. YES **NO**

2. Communication with a legislator or public official about personal assistance services. YES **NO**

3. Communication with a legislative aide about SB 144, The Personal Assistance Act of 1996. **(Telling which way to vote is lobbying)** YES **NO**

4. A letter to a senator, encouraging her to reject a nominee for Secretary of Education. **YES** NO

5. Communication to members of your center encouraging them to contact legislators regarding support for specific legislation. **YES** NO

6. Putting a notice in the local newspaper expressing the view of your organization regarding specific legislation. **YES** NO

7. Inviting a legislator to your center to educate him about issues of importance to people with disabilities. YES **NO**

8. Publishing an objective analysis of your community's public transportation plan in your newsletter. YES **NO**

9. Contact with a legislator regarding legislation which will effectively terminate your organization. YES **NO**

10. Contact with a legislator regarding a 20% cut in funding for your organization. **YES** NO

228

11. Endorsing a candidate for office who has been consistently supportive of independent living.   **YES**   NO

12. Surveying all candidates for a particular office and publishing the results in your local newspaper.   YES   **NO**

13. Attending a public hearing regarding pending legislation which will affect your organization.   YES   **NO**

14. Testifying at a public hearing at the written request of a legislative committee.   YES   **NO**

15. Sending an objective analysis of pending legislation to your members and five months later asking them to encourage legislators to vote against it.   **YES**   NO

16. Responding to a request for the state VR agency to encourage legislators to vote against a bill.   **YES**   NO

17. Providing transportation to the polls on election day.   YES   **NO**

18. Making postcards expressing support for pending legislation available on a table in the center's lobby.   **YES**   NO

19. Distributing a petition during skills training class that encourages your governor to look into housing needs in your state.   YES   **NO**

20. Putting a notice in the newspaper that your center is in favor of a referendum on the upcoming ballot.   **YES**   NO

Thanks

Thank you to everyone who helped me put together this book.

Thanks to the past and current staffs and boards of Arizona Bridge to Independent Living (ABIL) and Liberty Resources, Inc. (LRI).

Thanks to Kelly Boston who edited this book—a massive job because not only did she need first-rate editing skills and abundant grasp IL, but she also had to have the patience to put up with me.

Thanks to NCIL for its persistence and vision and adherence to its principles.

Thanks to Duane French for his kind words on the back cover.

Thanks to ILRU for its dedication to centers and SILCs.

Thanks to Loren Worthington and ABIL for the work they did on the book's cover.

Thanks to my brother, Jack, who first suggested that I write this book, then encouraged me throughout the process.

And finally, thank you to my wife, Ginger, whose love and support seems never-ending. I could not have done this without her.